Stellenbosch

To the memory of Rob Auld, a great friend
Daryl Balfour

Stellenbosch
place of gables, oaks & wine

photography
Daryl Balfour

text
Brian Johnson Barker

STRUIK

ACKNOWLEDGEMENTS

THE photography for this book was undertaken with the support and assistance of many people, to all of whom I am deeply grateful. David Hughes of Stellenbosch; Basie and Sandy Maartens of Mountain Shadows, Paarl; Rijk Melck and Kim Swemmer of Muratie Wine Farm; Norma and Stan Ratcliffe of Warwick Farm; Gert Lubbe of D'Ouwe Werf all offered both hospitality and sustenance during the months that this book was in preparation. My brother and his wife, Russell and Lee-Ann, and my niece and nephew, Michelle and Dylan, always provided a welcoming home for me in Cape Town, while on many occasions a peaceful getaway awaited me with my mother and Philip in Hermanus.

I should also like to express my appreciation to the many sponsors and supporters who make life easier for an itinerant photographer. In particular I am grateful to SA Canvas & Tent in Johannesburg; to Delta Motor Corporation; L. Saul & Co. Ltd.; Sean, Nina and Maia Beneke of Mhlume, Swaziland, and to John Matterson of Johannesburg. My thanks are also due to Struik Publishers of Cape Town and in particular to Peter Borchert, Eve Gracie, Neville Poulter, Marje Hemp and Christine Riley for their support and confidence over the past three years.

Finally, I am grateful to my wife, Sharna, without whom I could never have achieved so much nor realized so many dreams.

DARYL BALFOUR
Mhlume, March 1992

Half-title page *A cool arch frames a gable and greenery, a combination evocative of Stellenbosch.*
Title page *The greens of pines and vines clothe a hillside on Stellenzicht farm.*

Struik Publishers
(a member of The Struik Group (Pty) Ltd)
Cornelis Struik House
80 McKenzie Street
Cape Town 8001

Reg. No.: 63/00203/07

First published in 1992

Edited by Phillida Brooke Simons, Cape Town
Design by Jennifer Hoare, New Leaf Design, Cape Town
DTP conversion by BellSet, Cape Town
Typeset in Symbol ITC book 10pt
Reproduction by Unifoto (Pty) Ltd, Cape Town
Printed and bound by Leefung-Asco Printers Ltd, Hong Kong

ISBN 1 86825 149 7

CONTENTS

INTRODUCTION   6

DOWN THE YEARS   9

'THE FACE OF GOD'   43

THE TOWN OF OAKS   53

TO LEARN AND TO SERVE   75

THE PAST PRESERVED   97

AMONG THE VINES   105

SELECT BIBLIOGRAPHY   127

INDEX   129

Map of central Stellenbosch   55
Map of the Stellenbosch area, showing surrounding wine farms   128

Top *Mist over Stellenbosch, from Alto estate.*

Above *The National Monuments Council emblem, seen on many Stellenbosch buildings.*

INTRODUCTION

No matter where you may have come from you will find that Stellenbosch is unlike any other place on earth. In succeeding eras of change and modernization, the town has moved with the times without sacrificing too much of its substance or any of its soul.

Let us imagine that you have come from Cape Town, as so many of the town's visitors do, though your journey may have started in other parts of southern Africa or in lands beyond the seas. If you pause on a hill-slope to look back on your road, you may see Table Mountain in a perspective perhaps more pleasing than the view from immediately below its great, slab-sided walls. There are even a few born Capetonians – very few it is true – who say that on some days, mostly overcast, their mountain can seem just a little overpowering. In fact, in the 19th century, there were settlers in the eastern part of the province who spoke slightingly of 'gloomy Table Mountain politics', convinced that Cape Town's 'great, grey mother' exercised some perverse influence on those parliamentarians who sat in earnest debate beneath her cloud-wreathed crags.

But from the road to Stellenbosch, and there are several of them, Table Mountain and its outliers have, in a way, been restored to mere mortality as intriguing outlines on a departing horizon. Turn round and look ahead now, to other mountains. Perhaps you can see the hill that the early Dutch settlers called Klapmuts because it reminded them of an old-fashioned cap with earflaps. From another road you will see Helderberg, the clear mountain that protrudes from the circle of heights known for centuries as the Hottentots Holland. In the early years, Dutch explorers found groups here of the people once known as Hottentots but today more correctly called Khoikhoi or men of men. This place, explained the little pastoralists and hunters, was *their* home and, to make sure they were understood, may have alluded to it as *Hottentots' Holland*. They may have hoped that the Dutch would return all the way to their own Holland, but the dice of history were already loaded against them.

History is a relatively new idea in Stellenbosch, lying in the embrace of its mountains of Jonkershoek, Simonsberg, Drakenstein and others. Here is no brooding monolith; there are none of Kipling's 'aching Oudtshoorn ranges' but fold upon fold with gentle slopes and valleys, and jagged peaks of fable and legend. If mountains could sing, these, one feels, would burst into song. These are kindly mountains, with lower slopes that the farmer can till and plant, clothe with vines that are soft and shyly green in springtime and then, having borne their fruit, shed brown and gold and red before their winter sleep. It was beneath these mountains that history – which, so scholars say, is the written record of human events – awoke just a little over three centuries ago. But there are many ways of writing records, and prehistory here will take you back almost two million years. The Stellenbosch landscape then was fairly similar to what it is today. Primeval seas that had covered the land with a deep and fertile layer of alluvium had retreated. The Eerste River had made its way by several channels across the land, and rounded boulders and pebbles deposited by long-melted glaciers clashed and rolled on its stream bed as they still do when the river runs swiftly. In this way some of the record was written, but it was more closely defined by stone and its uses, especially these rounded river stones.

Perhaps it was Australopithecus, the 'southern ape', or the slightly later and more recognizably human *Homo habilis* – 'the handy man' – who discovered that by knocking two of these stones together a serviceable tool with a cutting or crushing edge could be produced. Another easily recognizable artefact of the times has come to be known as the 'hand axe', although it was probably far more versatile in application than we know. It is a pear-shaped stone, artificially trimmed and with a length of anything from about 15 to 30 cm or more. The sharp edges could be used for skinning or jointing an animal, the pointed end could have served for digging and the wide base would have been useful for crushing nuts, bones or roots. Many of these artefacts would have been made for an immediate use and then discarded when they had performed their task. Durable, and eloquent to the trained eye, they lay waiting in the earth that had long swallowed and digested their makers. For Australopithecus and *Homo habilis* both shambled their ways to extinction.

The good burghers of the Eerste River valley may have blunted their harrows and ploughshares on the implements so profusely scattered by their distant predecessors, but gave them little thought. The road-builder, Andrew Geddes Bain, has been termed the 'father' of archaeology and of palaeontology in South Africa because, before the middle of the 19th century, he recognized the fossils of extinct creatures for what they were. From the same period, another claimant to the title was the militant settler Thomas Holden Bowker who, like Bain, recognized stone artefacts found in the eastern part of the Cape Province. But neither of them, whatever the depth of their interest in oddities and curious things, can be said to have set South African archaeology on an academic footing. That happened at Stellenbosch.

It was on 18 March 1862 that the railway line reached Stellenbosch and the locomotive *Sir George Grey* steamed proudly into the station. On the approach from Cape Town the track cut through land owned by a farmer named Bosman whose name, in the form of Bosman's Crossing, had already been given to the drift, or ford, across the Plankenbrug River on the western approach to the town. Here a cutting had to be made for the track, and it was in the cutting, almost 40 years later – in 1899, when the railway station was known as Bosman's Siding – that the Director of the South African Museum in Cape Town, Dr Louis Peringuey, made the discovery that placed South African archaeology within the bounds of academic respectability. Some six metres below the original ground-surface, the walls of the cutting had exposed stone implements of a simple form and elementary workmanship

which Peringuey used to prove the great antiquity of the existence of human – or man-like – creatures in southern Africa. To this assemblage of implements and other artefacts, and to others later gathered here and elsewhere in the country, was given the name of Stellenbosch Culture. They date from the South African Earlier Stone Age, a period that lasted, with somewhat blurred edges, from about 1,2 million BC until around 200 000 years ago. However, the particular implements that characterized the Stellenbosch Culture were found not only in southern Africa but in other parts of the continent and, indeed, in many sites throughout much of the world.

Had Stellenbosch been the type-site, or the very first place where such implements were discovered and described, its name might have endured in the annals of archaeology. But the European type-site, which had been discovered much earlier, was in France, at a place called St Acheul. In Europe, implements that in South Africa were being assigned to the Stellenbosch Culture, were being described as belonging to the Acheulean tradition or phase of the Earlier Stone Age. And so, to toe the international academic line, Stellenbosch Culture was renamed to conform to the proponents of the early dweller of St Acheul. It seems a pity, but then academics are not noted for their sentimentality.

In the small, grassy triangle formed by Distillery and Adam Tas streets and the Plankenbrug River, is the Stellenbosch Geological Reserve. A rough stone monument embellished with

a bronze plaque ensures that neither Peringuey nor the Stellenbosch Culture will be forgotten, at any rate by those who trouble to examine the inscription. It reads: 'In a road maker's borrow pit here in 1899 Louis Peringuey made the first discovery of "Stellenbosch" stone implements and thereby proved the great antiquity of man in southern Africa.' Plaque and monument were placed there by the National Monuments Council, a statutory body whose emblem will be encountered on buildings in Stellenbosch over and over again.

Left Nobody knows who painted this charming picture.
This is the present Moederkerk, now much altered.

Above *The sandstone monument*
commemorating the Stellenbosch Culture.

DOWN THE YEARS

THE EERSTE RIVER, which lies at the very heart of Stellenbosch town and its story, is thought to have entered recorded history as long ago as 1655 when the Dutch settlement at the Cape of Good Hope was little more than three years old.

In September of that year Corporal Wilhelm Muller of the garrison was sent out by Commander Jan van Riebeeck to explore the unknown territory in the direction of 'the mountains of Africa' and, what was more important, to barter cattle from the tribespeople whom he might encounter. Muller, a slow and not entirely happy explorer, took all of 13 days to cross the Cape Flats and reach the shores of False Bay, a distance of some 50 km. On the way, the little band camped on the banks of a river somewhere in the vicinity of present-day Meerlust and, because it was the first stream they had encountered since leaving the Cape Peninsula, it later became known as the first or Eerste River. In similar imaginative fashion, the second river they crossed was called the 'Tweede' though this name lasted but a short while before it was changed to Lourens River. Muller, having lost most of the copper ingots he was supposed to trade for cattle, returned to the Fort of Good Hope empty-handed and once Van Riebeeck had recorded that disappointing fact, he never mentioned the corporal again in his daily journal. Muller disappeared from the record, but the Eerste River, joyously sparkling, flowed on.

There was little joy at the Fort of Good Hope, however, and not a great deal of sparkle. The colony had been planted at the Cape by Their High Mightinesses, the directors of the Dutch East India Company, to grow vegetables and obtain cattle to replenish the stores of ships trading between Europe and the East. Unfortunately, the settlement could not even feed itself and rice had to be sent regularly to the Cape from the Company's other possessions.

At this time the Dutch at the Cape were either Company servants or, after 1657, free burghers whose 'freedom', in practice, was somewhat limited. They were granted their independence not because of any generosity on the part of their employers but because this move saved money – the wages that the men would otherwise have been paid.

Because of this parsimonious attitude, expansion inland was slow and it was only in 1672 that an outpost

Left *Grass grows high around a tumbledown cottage under a fleecy winter sky.*

Below right *Smooth and water-worn stones form the bed of the Eerste River as it flashes and sparkles its way through the town.*

was established at Hottentots Holland, near present-day Somerset West, where wheat was grown on a small scale. Then, in August of 1679, Henning Hüsing and Claas Gerrits, former Company shepherds on their way to becoming cattle barons, were granted permission to graze their flocks and herds between the Eerste River and Hottentots Holland. Two months later, on 12 October, there arrived in Table Bay the new commander of the Cape settlement, an energetic and enterprising man named Simon van der Stel.

WHO WAS SIMON VAN DER STEL?

According to Peter Kolb, the German traveller, astronomer, botanist and from 1711 secretary to the college of landdrost and heemraden of Stellenbosch, he was the son of a black slave woman. But Kolb disliked the Van der Stels, especially Simon's son Wilhem Adriaen, and so was happy to put about a story that might have been considered mildly scandalous. In fact, it

was Simon's grandmother, Monica Dacosta – Monica of the coast – who may have been a slave, but there is no certainty of this. She came from the Coromandel coast of India, and was, in all probability, Eurasian.

Born at sea in 1639 near the island of Mauritius where his father became commander, Simon van der Stel was orphaned young. He travelled to Holland in 1660, and, as was customary, the return fleet called for provisions at Table Bay. Here, during the weeks that the ships lay at anchor in the roadstead, Van der Stel must have explored the little settlement and perhaps formed the ambition of returning one day to build it into a new Dutch colony. In Holland, he acquired an excellent knowledge of Latin, chemistry, and farming – especially viticulture and winemaking. He also acquired a wife, Johanna Six, a daughter of the influential mayor of Amsterdam. Although it produced no fewer than six children, theirs was not the happiest of marriages, the relationship between Simon and his wife even giving rise to an action for libel. Not surprisingly, when he left to take up his new appointment, wife Johanna elected to stay behind in Holland, although all of their children, as well as his wife's youngest sister, Cornelia, and two cousins set sail with Simon aboard the ship *Vrije Zee*. Husband and wife never met again, and probably never regretted it.

Once he had arrived at the Cape, Van der Stel – more than almost any other of the colony's commanders or governors – set out to make it a materially better place for European settlement. During his years there he attempted to exploit the copper deposits of Namaqualand and enthusiastically encouraged the implementation of better farming methods. He went farming himself, at his estate of Constantia which is more likely to have been named for the virtue of constancy than – as has been suggested – in honour of the child of some high official. His creation of the sub-colony of Stellenbosch was not by order of the Company, but an act prompted by something within himself, something that one is tempted to think was a love for this new land.

Perhaps the surest evidence of his love for the Cape, and one of his more endearing acts, is his decision to remain here after retiring in 1699 with the rank of governor. Previously, the only other commanders or governors to stay at the Cape were those who had died in office, but Simon van der Stel actually chose to remain. He was buried in Cape Town's Groote Kerk, then the *Nieuwe Kerk*, under whose floor his dust mingles with that of the land he loved so well.

THE FOUNDING OF THE TOWN

Less than a month after his arrival Simon van der Stel set out to explore his domain, especially the post at distant Hottentots Holland. It was a modest journey but it was to put the name of Stellenbosch on the map of the interior – a map that had few enough names anyway and scarcely any accurately plotted features. 'Besides the herewith mentioned region of Hottentots Holland,' wrote his scribe, 'His Excellency also went to view a certain region which is situated about three to four hours from it. It consists of a level valley with several thousand morgen of beautiful pasturage, also very suitable for agriculture. Through the valley flows a very impressive freshwater river with its banks fringed by beautiful tall trees and these trees are very suitable both for timber and fuel. In the river a small island was discovered around which the water streams and which is densely overgrown with beautiful high trees. There the honourable Commander took his night's rest and as no one in authority had ever been there before, he called it Stellenbosch.' And for a while, Stellenbosch was to remain no more than a name.

Looking at the Eerste River in the town of Stellenbosch today, one finds it difficult to picture an island of a size sufficient to accommodate an early Cape commander and his entourage. But this is indeed the river, and the old island of Stellenbosch is today occupied, in part, by the Theological Seminary. The river, when the Commander's party reached it, was divided into two channels: one followed the course that the Eerste River still takes on its way through Stellenbosch and the other, northerly, channel swung out to enclose a large, teardrop-shaped piece of land – the island – before rejoining the main flow less than midway down the present Dorp Street.

That it was the island to which he gave his name, and not the district is clear from the record. On the land grants that show the Eerste River, it is only the island itself that is named Stellenbosch and the first settlers referred to themselves not as residents of Stellenbosch but as being of the 'colony on the banks of the Eerste River'.

Tradition and early historians assert that the first settler in the new colony moved there in the same year of 1679 but, if this is so, his name has been lost. However, in May of the next year, eight families arrived, and some 15 or 16 more in 1682. Within five years of proclamation, many farms along the Eerste River, with names still well known today, had been granted. These included Blaauwklip (granted to G J Vischer), Coetsenburg (Dirck Coetse), Jonkershoek (Jan de Jonker), Libertas (Jan Cornelisz, also known as Jan Bombam), Mostertsdrif (J C Mostert), Schoongezicht, later known as Lanzerac (I Schrijver),

and Welgevallen (J S Botma). Among these pioneer farmers were a number of men belonging to the class accorded the status of 'free black'. Although the term 'Vrij Swart' was also used in the Dutch possessions in the East and included several classes of people, at the Cape it referred only to freed slaves some of whom, in order to work their properties to the best advantage, became slave owners themselves. Those free blacks who were granted land in the new colony, all of it in the Jonkershoek area, included Jan and Marquard of Ceylon who received Weltevreden (now Old Nectar), Louis of Bengal (Leef-op-Hoop, later Klein Gustrow) and Antonie of Angola.

The first harvest, in 1690, showed that Simon van der Stel had not been misguided in establishing this new farming community. No fewer than 400 muids – about 36 400 kg – of wheat were brought in and, within three years, the figure had risen to slightly more than 3 000 (273 000 kg). In 1689, just before the first Stellenbosch farms were established, 'the Cape' had produced a total of 1 750 muids, so the new colony very soon justified its existence and the Commander's judgement. Although it had no formal boundaries, Stellenbosch came to be understood as not just the island in the river but any area outside the confines of the Cape Peninsula. Not only were there no boundaries, there was no town.

To have founded a village, or to have up-graded an outpost to village status, would have cost the Company money and Van der Stel knew how it would feel about that. Thus, instead of *creating* the village itself, he had set up the circumstances to provide the *need* for one or, at the very least, for a centre for administration and worship. And, what would please the Company, this village would be virtually self-funding.

It was the Company's obsession with profit and, in particular, its determination to stamp out *morshandel* – private or wasteful trading – among its servants, that eventually provided the opportunity for the founding of Stellenbosch village. To investigate financial misdoings throughout its Empire, the Dutch East India Company appointed a former governor of Malabar, Hendrik van Reede tot Drakestein who, with the rank of commissioner-general and wielding vast powers, arrived at the Cape in April of 1685. With another high official, Baron St Martin, and escorted by Simon van der Stel himself, the Commissioner-General visited all the outposts of the Company in this far corner of Africa. According to one account, they reached the site of the future town of Stellenbosch in pouring rain, and Van der Stel was disappointed that, from the foot of Hagelsberg (now Papegaaiberg), they were unable to see the splendour of the surrounding mountains. They were, though, able to discern the thin scatter of white, limewashed and thatched dwellings of the burghers dotting the countryside. Precisely when Van Reede took the decision that a village should be established on the level plain beside the Eerste River is not certain, but in this regard he left clear instructions for Commander van der Stel when he sailed from the Cape in July.

On broad topics, the Commissioner-General expressed the wish that many more trees – particularly oaks – should be planted. He recommended that further vineyards should be established and he had some firm opinions on the construction of buildings at the Company's outposts – opinions, so it turned out, that greatly influenced the future trend of Cape architecture. And then Van Reede got down to the matter of Stellenbosch itself. In the first place, it appeared to him that insufficient thought had been given to planning the settlement: some farms, he noticed, were separated by great distances while others were crowded together and yet others seemed to possess far more than their fair share of river bank. By way of a mild rebuke, Van Reede expressed the view that the best interests of the Company would have been served not by free burghers but by settling paid officials as farmers. This must have surprised Van der Stel in view of the evidence provided by the improved wheat harvest, that free burghers appeared to apply themselves more diligently than Company servants. However, Van Reede conceded that as matters had already developed considerably, he would not change the system.

Comments made by Van Reede again stress the Company's sole concern with the promotion of profitable trade, not with colonization. Company officials would work the soil merely because they were paid to do so whereas free burghers would identify themselves not only with the soil but with the land, with the country itself. They might even, in time, come to think of themselves more as Africans than as Hollanders. However, as it was on this visit that Van Reede confirmed the grant to Van der Stel of the glorious Constantia estate, it is unlikely that there were any serious differences between Commissioner-General and Commander. Rather, it would seem that Van Reede was infected by some of Van der Stel's enthusiasm for Stellenbosch for he declared that its burgher-farmers should remain where they were and not seek to be re-absorbed into the community at the Castle. Stellenbosch was to be a separate district, a purely agricultural colony which he acknowledged 'might become in time a very beautiful place'.

A good bureaucrat, Van Reede made provisions for the burghers' immediate needs. Firstly, he ordained that local government at Stellenbosch should consist of a magistrate, or landdrost and his advisers, or heemraden. A court house or drostdy was to be built to serve also as the landdrost's residence and with a room in which the ordinary meetings with his heemraden might be held. Van Reede even determined the site on which the drostdy should be built: it was to be on 'the tiny island called Stellenbosch'. The building of a church could be delayed, although its position was already earmarked.

There was already a schoolmaster of sorts, in the rather sad figure of Sijbrand Mancadan, a broken-down former minister of religion who served also as sick-comforter.

Left and far left *Stellenbosch abounds in good venues for drink and food – and friendship.*

Right *Charming Mon Repos cottage was given its name by a French owner who had difficulty pronouncing its earlier title of Onder-Papegaaiberg.*

In time, so Van Reede foresaw, it would be necessary to lay out building plots and make of the 'wagon-road to the Cape' an attractive street, with 'one house next to the other' and facing the Eerste River from which the occupants would irrigate their kitchen gardens. These houses did eventually come to be built but, as a walk along Dorp Street shows, they were erected relatively far from the river and, instead of facing it, fronted the street. Van Reede's vision of a Dutch river-town, when it came into being, was created in the local idiom, rather than as a faithful copy of 'home'.

Meanwhile, left with a sheaf of instructions and also with permission to undertake an expedition to the north in search of payable copper deposits, Van der Stel opted for the grand adventure to Namaqualand. This delayed operations in Stellenbosch until 1686 when the Commander visited the settlement on 29 July to commission the building of the 'houses of God and of the Company'. First to be completed was the drostdy, while the laying-out of the church site created the first street crossing in the village, later to become the intersection of Ryneveld and Church streets. It is here that the town's oldest dwellings are to be seen, among them Schreuderhuis dating from about 1709 and now part of the Village Museum.

Simon van der Stel's next visit to Stellenbosch was on his birthday, 14 October 1686. Contrary to popular belief, the Commander did not make a regular habit of visiting 'his' village as part of his birthday celebrations. His movements and travels were well recorded at the time and, of 33 birthdays that he celebrated in southern Africa, on only three of them did he visit Stellenbosch. On this, his first birthday-visit, he was annoyed to discover how slow the progress of the builders had been. But by mid-April 1687 the drostdy was ready to be occupied by its first incumbent, Johannes Mulder of Rotterdam.

Above *Vines take on the russet shades of advancing autumn. By the end of March, most of the grape crop has been harvested, and the vines will be pruned in June. Vines in commercial vineyards may live for up to 30 years, grapes for wine-making being borne from about the sixth year.*

Right *Light, shade and the stark limbs of a gum tree lend a three-dimensional quality to this pastoral evening scene. There are pines here too, and these and other fast-growing exotics are often planted as windbreaks. In some areas, unfortunately, they have become naturalized and spread beyond control, disturbing the natural balance.*

16

Mulder had arrived at the Cape five years earlier, as a Company's soldier aboard the *Geele Beer*. Ashore, he was appointed storekeeper but was dismissed for criticizing an officer, the Company being touchy about matters of rank and privilege. Jobless and, he claimed, homeless, Mulder appealed to Commissioner-General van Reede tot Drakestein who appointed him to the newly created post of landdrost of Stellenbosch. Later to become a free burgher and prosperous farmer, Mulder was to serve a second spell as landdrost of Stellenbosch after much of the village had been destroyed by fire in 1710. The extensive farms he owned were in the area that is still known as Muldersvlei.

Soon after the commencement of Mulder's drostdy, attention was turned to the church which had troubles of its own to contend with. Soldier and adventurer Oloff Bergh was in charge of supplying timber for its construction and complained that not only did he have insufficient wagons to fetch it from the slopes of the Hottentots Holland Mountains, but those that he did possess were too old to manage the rough tracks. (This Lieutenant Bergh was an ancestor of the O M Bergh whose elegant 19th-century home is now a part of the Village Museum.) The wagons had been borrowed from the local burghers who were understandably indignant about the way in which their property was being battered about on the mountainsides. To their great relief, Van der Stel eventually gave Bergh permission to use Company transport.

The cornerstone of the church was laid on 14 February 1687 although the first full service had been held in the house of one of the burghers on 13 October 1686, the day before Van der Stel's birthday. The preacher on this occasion had been the Reverend Johannes Overneij whose dearest wish it was to administer Holy Communion in the completed church of Stellenbosch. Sad to relate, he died early in May, just before it was completed, leaving a 'pregnant and sorrowing housewife, with five children'. The original Stellenbosch church, of which now only the foundations remain within the cellar of a later building, was the first permanent Christian place of worship to be built in South Africa.

It must be admitted that the earliest citizens of Stellenbosch were by no means the cultural cream of the Cape. The church at that time was a much more powerful influence for order and discipline than it is today, but in Stellenbosch it was failed by its representative, the unfortunate Sijbrand Mancadan. Although his responsibility as a husband and, soon, as a father, prompted him to try to rehabilitate himself, he received no help or encouragement from the burghers. Many of them refused

Left *Mist-softened sunlight strikes one of the peaks in the range that holds town and winelands in its gentle embrace.*

Above *With leaves showing the tints of autumn, this distant relative of the grape vine trails over a wall in Stellenbosch.*

Below *In appearance quite unlike the older Cape Dutch dwellings, Victorian houses have nevertheless mellowed graciously on many Stellenbosch streets. The most striking group is to be seen in the vicinity of Van Riebeeck Street where names, thought to be the original ones, range from Bonne Espérance to Heemstede and Lichfield. Turrets and turnip domes, cast-iron and pre-produced mouldings, all are in evidence here.*

Right *A delivery cycle, an increasingly rare sight in South Africa, is unselfconsciously at home on a Stellenbosch stoep.*

to allow their children to be taught by him and they shunned the services he held. They even turned him from their doors when he called, as he was obliged to do, to comfort the sick by reading to them from the scriptures.

Despite his failings and weaknesses, Mancadan was retained as secretary to the landdrost and heemraden and also as sick-comforter. He lasted as secretary until 1691 but in 1694 the muster rolls record the name of Jan Jansz Swart as sick-comforter for Stellenbosch. Mancadan's ultimate fate is unknown but it is presumed that he must have died in that year or the year before. That he had failed was perhaps not entirely his own fault for even the authorities at the Castle considered many of the Stellenbosch burghers to be 'rough customers'. But this is often the case with pioneers.

HUGUENOTS AND OTHERS

An important aspect of the establishment of the town in terms of Van Reede's instructions was the direct participation of members of the community in their government. Thus, with its 'college' of landdrost and heemraden, Stellenbosch became the first model of local government. There was the potential for a greater degree of true democracy to be found in the new colony than in the mother-settlement on Table Bay. There, government was entirely by Company officials.

The college of landdrost and heemraden had been devised in Batavia and was based on the Dutch rural court system of bailiff and high-born gentry. The first Cape heemraden, those of Stellenbosch, had in fact been appointed even before the landdrost – in 1682. They were Hendrick Elbertsz, Hans Jurgen Grimpe, Henning Hüsing and Gerrit van der Bijl. In later years it was usual for a landdrost to be assisted by six heemraden, half of whom retired each year. Before this occurred, however, the full college of landdrost and heemraden submitted to the commander or governor a list of names so that when he chose the replacements they were thus not entirely 'governor's men'. Heemraden received no pay; had to be at least 30 years old and in possession of fixed property. Their duties included the resolution of property disputes and the provision and maintenance of roads and water supplies.

As a buffer zone between the Cape Peninsula and the interior, Stellenbosch urgently required military organization of some kind, but Van Reede merely instructed the new landdrost, Johannes Mulder, to requisition free burghers and instruct officials to be on the alert against enemies of the Company and other such 'rogues' and, if required, to arrest them. By a decision of the Council of Policy on 5 August 1685 the

landdrost and heemraden were also made responsible for the defence of their little colony.

In July of the next year Van der Stel established the local burgher militia by appointing officers, an ensign and a sergeant who, when he visited his village a few months later, greeted him by firing three salvos from their long, smoothbore muskets. The performance was repeated on the Commander's birthday a few days later when no fewer than 88 men paraded. The first officers were none other than the heemraden, with the addition of Jan Mostert as ensign of the company of infantry and Pieter van der Bijl as ensign of the troop of dragoons. For so young a colony, the turnout was impressive and the numbers were to become even more so when they were swelled in 1688 by the addition of French Huguenot refugees.

In selecting new settlers from among the French refugees, the Dutch East India Company looked particularly for 'those who are cultivators of the vine and understand the making of vinegar and the distillation of brandy…' In the event, very few of the refugees did possess any of this desirable knowledge or experience and their contribution to improving the quality of Cape wine has generally been exaggerated. But they did make good burghers, although an early entry in Van der Stel's journal suggests that not all were as industrious as he had hoped. They were settled among the Dutch, mainly along the Berg River, but also at Drakenstein and Olifantshoek which, in time, became known as De Fransche Hoek. They brought with them their own clergyman, the Reverend Pierre Simond, who was

granted two farms in the area and instructed to preach, on alternate Sundays, at Drakenstein and Stellenbosch. A number of the refugees also settled at Stellenbosch itself or moved there during the course of the next decade or so. They included Jean Prieur du Plessis, a physician, Guillaume du Toit, Guillaume Niel (whose surname was to become Nel) and, later, Jacques Malan and Antonie Faure.

Within a few decades the French language faded away, official proclamations appearing in both French and Dutch only until 1697. A few years later the Reverend Henricus Beck, who had replaced Simond, was instructed that he was no longer to preach in French and French instruction in school was also forbidden. But what finally brought about the swift and complete integration of the French with the Dutch was their opposition to an unpopular overlord, Wilhem Adriaen, the son of Simon van der Stel.

Old Simon had been elevated to the (better-paid) rank of governor in 1691 and in 1699 he retired to enjoy his last years on his country estate of Constantia. It must have been a particular pleasure to him to be able to induct as the next governor his eldest son, then aged 35 years. In his teens, the younger Van der Stel had been employed at the Castle as an assistant writer and, later, as quartermaster. Then, in 1684, he sailed for Holland aboard the *Europa*, and in the same year married Maria de Hase, daughter of an important Company official. Wilhem Adriaen prospered in Amsterdam and, as a well-respected community member, became churchwarden and alderman before he was appointed to succeed his father.

Like his father, Wilhem Adriaen was able and enthusiastic, but with not nearly so much good luck. Daniel Heins, one of the Company's commissioners who visited the Cape soon after Wilhem Adriaen's arrival, granted senior officials tracts of farmland and also plots in the slowly growing town around the Castle. The Van der Stels came in for more than their fair share, Simon receiving still more land to add to his already vast holdings at Constantia, Wilhem being granted farmland at Hottentots Holland and his brother, Frans, also getting a generous acreage in the area. In a very short time, the Van der Stel family, father and sons, owned most of the farming area of Hottentots Holland or, if they did not actually own it, certainly treated it as their private preserve. The brothers, whose lands adjoined each other, started farming on an impressive scale that did not go unnoticed, especially by the resentful burghers of nearby Stellenbosch. To their chagrin they were even forbidden to fish in False Bay south of the Lourens River and watched with growing indignation as Wilhem Adriaen

Left *An ornately fringed veranda shades the symmetry of a town-house façade.*

Right *A light dusting of fallen leaves lies on the lawn at Blaauwklippen, built around 1790 by Dirk Hoffman and today one of the attractions on the Stellenbosch Wine Route. From October to Easter, visitors are shown the vineyards from the delightful vantage point of a horse-drawn carriage.*

expanded his estate, which he named Vergelegen, until it was more than 10 times the size of the average holding.

The year 1705 was a bad one for the burghers. Van der Stel awarded the wine contract to one of his cronies and, a few months later, made the foolish move of withdrawing the meat contract from Henning Hüsing of Meerlust. With his nephew, Adam Tas, who had married the Widow Grimpe of the farm Libertas, Hüsing decided to take action.

Tas had arrived at the Cape in 1697 as a free burgher and worked for his uncle Hüsing at Meerlust as secretary and bookkeeper before marrying the wealthy widow and becoming a Stellenbosch farmer of some substance. In common with other free burghers, he found himself increasingly unable to compete with the Company officials who manipulated contracts and markets to suit themselves. Tas, who had considerable literary ability, was asked to draw up a memorandum setting out the burghers' complaints against Van der Stel and

his officials, and this memorandum was later read to groups of free burghers who, if they agreed with its contents, signed a petition of affirmation. Word of this action reached the Governor and, soon, so too did a copy of Tas's memorandum.

The landdrost of Stellenbosch at this time was Johannes Starrenburgh. Since it was Wilhem Adriaen van der Stel who had appointed him to his post, Starrenburgh was, not surprisingly, one of his supporters. In fact, he frequently appealed to him for support and at the height of the scandal asked to be protected from the wrath of the Stellenbosch burghers. It was Starrenburgh who, at the head of a posse of soldiers, arrested Tas at Libertas in February 1706 and took him, as well as his writing desk, to the Castle where he was placed in the dungeon and his desk carefully emptied. The desk yielded what was described as 'malicious writing', including a diary in which unflattering references were made to a great many Cape people, both Company officials and burghers. This provided

Wilhem Adriaen with the evidence he needed of what he re-garded as disloyalty; he promptly drew up a counter-document in which he justified his own conduct and that of his officials. To Starrenburgh he gave the rather wretched job of collecting signatures in support of his claims, a task that the obsequious landdrost seems to have tackled with enthusiasm. In the course of going his rounds in Stellenbosch, Starrenburgh clashed outside the mill at the upper end of today's Dorp Street with a young man named Hendrik Bibault and there threatened him with the force of his authority. However, Bibault, in refusing to obey an order to 'move along', made what has come to be regarded as a historic reply when he said (in part), 'Ik wil niet loopen, ik ben een Africaander…' This is the first recorded occasion on which anyone called himself an 'Afrikaner'.

Meanwhile, in faraway Amsterdam, Their High Mightinesses The Lords Seventeen studied Tas's memorandum along with other important documents. They must, one feels, have known what was coming and Wilhem Adriaen van der Stel, together with Starrenburgh and other senior officials, was recalled to Holland. It is interesting to note that Starrenburgh's wife and her five children from a previous marriage did not accompany the discredited former landdrost when he was exiled but elected to stay at the Cape. Whether family ties had loosened over the scandal or there were shades of the parting of Simon van der Stel from Johanna Six, one does not know.

Wilhem Adriaen's wife, Maria de Hase, returned to Holland with her husband although, if the diary of Adam Tas is to be believed, love had either died or certainly been placed under tremendous strain. This is what he wrote: 'They tell me that the Governor's wife had, in a fit of despondency, tried to drown herself by jumping into the fountain behind the house at the Cape. Mrs Berg was on the spot and ran to help her, pulling her out of the water, to whom the Governor's wife lamented bitterly that her life had become one of terror for her on account of the many scandalous acts she must daily bear and witness.'

Tas was released, and joyfully returned to Libertas. (It is often claimed that he chose the name at this time, the pun 'Tas is free' being especially appropriate, but the farm had been known as Libertas even before he became the owner. It is a good story, though.)

With the order for Wilhem Adriaen to return to Holland, there arrived another which banned his brother Frans from the Company's territories for life. The mighty had indeed fallen, although Wilhem Adriaen tried to use his influential friends to obtain permission to remain at the Cape, even as an ordinary burgher. Whatever his shortcomings, he seems, like his father, to have genuinely loved the land but the Lords Seventeen were firm. Vergelegen was to be divided into four portions and sold and the homestead was to be demolished. Charges and counter-charges were published in Holland, but Wilhem Adriaen van der Stel never returned to the Cape. He did, though, live the leisured life of a gentleman of means and died at Lisse in 1733. His father, old Simon, predeceased him by some 21 years, living in peace and absorbed in agriculture at Constantia. What he thought of his son's conduct nobody knows, but he does not seem to have interfered in government once he had handed over to his son.

Freed from the tyranny of misgovernment, the good burghers of Stellenbosch and the other little settlements could look forward to better times.

Far left *Saturday is flea-market day in Stellenbosch, and there's no telling what you might find on the bright, busy stalls.*

Left *The Stellenbosch Food and Wine Festival is an occasion upon which to celebrate some of life's good things. This annual event, held late in October, has quickly gained a reputation for excellence.*

Right *Church House in Drostdy Street, once the Utopia Home for elderly ladies, is now the offices of the Dutch Reformed Church.*

FIRE AND SILVER

Appealing as the town is today, the tiny village of Stellenbosch also proved attractive to visiting artists almost three centuries ago. The earliest picture, a drawing dated 15 February 1710 by E V de Stade, shows what is very obviously a pioneer settlement. There is no neat alignment of houses and the buildings depicted are devoid of any decorative frills. The few gables that appear are at the house-ends and are strictly functional, usually carrying a chimney. Other chimneys poke through the simple, thatched roofs of square or oblong little houses. Window openings are few, and it is doubtful whether many of them were protected by glass.

The first church stands within a boundary of straggling hedge and is the largest building. Behind it and slightly obscured is the simple cottage that is Schreuderhuis, today a part of the Village Museum. The builder of this house at the corner of what have become Church and Ryneveld streets was Sebastiaan Schreuder who, at the time the drawing was made, was messenger of the local court. A German, Schreuder came to the Cape as a soldier in the service of the Dutch East India Company in about 1707 and soon afterwards was appointed as secretary to the public mill at Stellenbosch. The mill can be seen in the Van Stade drawing at the far end of the thoroughfare that has become Dorp Street, and an older mill building, already disused, is somewhat apart and to the left of the picture. This became Oude Molen farm.

Schreuder married Sara Wijnsandt, a widow, in 1710 and the couple lived in the modest house he had built the year before. In August 1711 he requested permission to resign his office because he wished to leave the Cape and within a few months the little house had been sold to a local farmer, Abraham Everts, and Sebastiaan and Sara Schreuder had sailed away to Europe where their subsequent fortunes remain largely unknown. By then, Stellenbosch as they had known it, and as Van Stade had depicted it, was no more.

December 1710 was a month of heat and wind. The seasonal south-easter blew with greater than usual force, buffeting the sentries on the ramparts of the Castle where the journal entry for Wednesday 17 December told a sad tale. 'News arrived this morning from Stellenbosch where, yesterday forenoon at about 10 o'clock, there broke out a fierce fire which has destroyed the council house, the church, the Company's store and laid another twelve houses in ashes. It would appear the fire was the result of a sorrowful accident...'

A special commission was immediately sent to Stellenbosch to determine the cause of the fire and, almost as important,

who should be punished for it. First suspicion, as ever, fell on the slaves. Like all slave-owning communities, the people of Stellenbosch had to be constantly on their guard against acts of desperation by those whom they had deprived of freedom and turned into mere units of labour. But the commission, despite the anxious assistance of landdrost Samuel Martini de Meurs, could reach no conclusion beyond the fact that the fire seemed to have started in the roof of the council house. Peter Kolb told a different tale: he asserted that the guilty party was none other than the landdrost himself. Seated in the office of the council house or drostdy on the day of the fire, De Meurs decided he would like to smoke his pipe and so sent a slave to the kitchen to fetch live coals from the stove. As the slave emerged from the kitchen with a container of glowing embers, a blast of wind through the open courtyard sent a shower of sparks on to the thatched roof which, in an instant, was blazing fiercely. Aided by the gale-force wind – it was reported of this windy spell that streets were 'almost unusable' – the fire leapt to the Company's store, and then across the north channel of the Eerste River to the house of Andries Pietersz and on down the little row of modest dwellings of the Van den Berg, Swart and Van Wijk families. A few gusts more and the house of Sebastiaan Schreuder was ablaze and so, too, was the church. (During 20th-century restoration of Schreuderhuis, evidence of repairs to fire damage was found in the front wall.)

It is possible that straw, as well as reed, was used to thatch the roofs which burnt furiously as lumps of lighted thatching lifted off and were carried away on the wind. The oaks suffered

Left *The trees are leafless, and white walls are stark in wintry Dorp Street.*

Right *The Herte Street cottages have been home to an assortment of residents over the years. These, perhaps, are the most colourful.*

badly in the blaze, too, and a thousand or so young trees were ordered from the Company's forest at Rondebosch to replace them. Landdrost de Meurs was soon replaced, too, by the popular Johannes Mulder who had served as first landdrost after the founding of the settlement. De Meurs, perhaps weighed down by guilt at the calamity he had unwittingly caused, died a few years after the fire at a fairly young age.

Plans were soon in hand for the rebuilding of the town. The Council of Policy at the Castle decreed that free wood should be given to help with repairing the damaged houses and also formulated new fire regulations for the entire Cape settlement. The drostdy was immediately rebuilt on its old site on the 'island' but no start was made on the ruins of the church which, season by season, eroded away ever more. Burghers restoring their houses were warned not to use straw, and the earliest record of a flat, tiled roof, albeit in Cape Town, dates from 1717. Furrows, to which water could be led from the river, were dug in front of the existing houses and from it the tank of a newly acquired 'fire engine', a hand-operated and hand-drawn pump, could be filled by means of leather buckets.

Dry summer thatch and the south-easter were a deadly combination and it is surprising that some 25 years were to pass before the landdrost, then Pieter Lourens, decided to do something about eliminating the more obvious risks. In 1736 he declared that he was concerned at the number of people, drunk and sober, who walked the streets carrying some or other lighted material. With the permission of Governor Jan de la Fontaine placards were erected declaring it illegal to smoke in the street or to carry about fire in any form. The severity of the punishment depended on the identity of the offender rather than on the gravity of his misdeed. Burghers were fined 15 rix dollars, Company servants lost two months' salary while slaves and 'Hottentots' were ordered to be flogged. To assist the landdrost to implement these and other laws, a sort of police official known as a veldwachter was appointed and, at the time of the post-fire rebuilding, the town's amenities were improved by the erection of the first gaol. There is a tale that after two convicts escaped, the gaoler, pleading in his own defence, declared that he could not be held responsible for their escape as the doors had no locks.

By 1750, according to the rambling memoirs of Petrus Borchardus Borcherds, the population of the Stellenbosch district had increased to 3 933 people of all classes. There were some 14 000 head of cattle, 72 000 sheep but only 136 pigs. More than two million vines had been planted which in that year produced 1 732 707 litres of wine. But the district of

This avenue is part of the quiet country road to Devon Valley below the slopes of the Bottelaryberg. Aboard ships of the Dutch East India Company the bottelary was the provision store and the name may have been applied locally because hay produced here on a large scale was issued to farmers in other districts.

Stellenbosch, for which Borcherds quotes the figures, bore no resemblance to the magisterial district of Stellenbosch today. The Cape district was a strip of land and coast from St Helena Bay to False Bay, while the district of Stellenbosch, bounded by the line of the Mosselbank and Kuils rivers laid down in 1711 and undefined to the north and east, seems to have been the rest of Africa. In practice, which was difficult enough to observe, the authority of the Stellenbosch landdrost extended wherever there were white people in the interior. And as they travelled further and further from the Cape settlement, so did the district of Stellenbosch expand to proportions impossible to administer. Eventually, with the creation of the drostdy of Swellendam in 1745, a large stretch of country was excised from the district of Stellenbosch. At full stretch, in about 1780, Stellenbosch extended from the mouth of the Buffels River, close to the modern diamond-mining settlement of Kleinsee in Namaqualand, eastwards to the Great Fish River. To the north, the boundary was a rough line along the Kamiesberg, Hantam, Nuweveld and Sneeuberg ranges. It was clearly impossible to control so vast an area and, with the creation of new districts – starting with Graaff-Reinet in 1786 – that of Stellenbosch was progressively reduced to a manageable size. In 1839 it lost the districts of Wynberg, Malmesbury, Paarl and Caledon, achieving its present proportions only after 1900 when Bellville and Somerset West became separate magistracies.

Whatever the size of the district of Stellenbosch, its heart lay in its village and the surrounding farmland, with administration still centred in the drostdy on its little island. It was a pretty village, of green trees, cultivated fields and wide roadways with thatched and white-washed houses at peace within the enfolding ring of mountains. We know this because in 1757 an artist visited Stellenbosch. (A few years earlier a French visitor had described the place as consisting of 30 houses and a church, but he left no drawing or painting.) The artist's name is unknown, but copies of two pictures that he – or she – painted are in the Village Museum. One shows the church on a new site chosen after the fire of 1710, and, peeping through the foliage of a lane of oaks that is Drostdy Street, the drostdy itself. It appears to be a single-storeyed building having a front façade with windows symmetrically arranged on either side of a central door. A tall, very simple gable has a window, presumably to light an attic; that of the nearby parsonage is more elaborate but the remainder of the houses are plain, workmanlike boxes – snug enough, no doubt, but quite unpretentious.

The artist folded his easel, put away his paints and departed. Five years later the drostdy that he had recorded was in flames.

Left *Now an art gallery, Libertas Parva in Dorp Street is a classic H-shaped building with two separate front doors. This was once the home of the Krige family whose daughter, Sybella, married Jan Smuts, future Prime Minister of South Africa.*

Above *Very much a Victorian afterthought, but attractive for all that, is this little Dorp Street veranda.*

Once again it was rebuilt, given an 'H' floor plan and a wonderfully ornate gable set in a façade probably unrivalled at the time for its beauty and symmetry. That this building has vanished was not due to yet another fire but to its being incorporated into the present Theological Seminary.

The loss of the second drostdy prompted the importation from Holland of a new fire-engine, partly paid for by the church council which, apart from the church itself and the parsonage, was responsible for a number of other buildings. Two fire-wardens, Johannes Victor and Lambertus Fick, were appointed and each had two assistants. They were to inspect buildings in the town and take particular note of chimneys they considered to be dangerous. A common cause of fire in thatched roofs was a ridge pole loosely built into a chimney and protruding into the flue; now householders could be ordered to break theirs down if necessary and reconstruct them to the satisfaction of the fire-wardens. Then, in 1803, came a published list of some 20 regulations for the better prevention and fighting of fires, but no number of rules could offer protection against one that was deliberately started.

On the morning of 28 December 1803, which had started with a mild south-easter, the Ryneveld Street shop and stable of wagon-builder Jacob Kuhl went up in flames. The fire-brigade was called out but their exertions proved in vain and a second alarm was given soon after they had dispersed. The brigade's new efforts were doomed to be fruitless too, because by now the wind speed had accelerated and, from somewhere near the east end of Dorp Street close to the corner of Ryneveld Street, the fire ran rampant. In a widening swathe of disaster reaching as far as Market Street, '42 houses as well as other buildings were quickly reduced to ashes'.

Investigators soon found evidence of arson. The first place to yield clues was the property of C E Ackerman, now the site of Hauptfleisch House (153 Dorp Street). In the stable charred fragments of woollen cloth were found, and in a nearby garden more burnt pieces of clothing were discovered as well as a bamboo pole smeared with a fatty substance. This and other evidence led to a woman recorded only as Julia and a slave called Patientie. Tried and found guilty at Cape Town, they were brought back to Stellenbosch to be publicly hanged.

With money raised by the Batavian Government (using the simple expedient of printing a mass of banknotes) and loaned interest-free to those who had lost their properties, the village was again rebuilt. This was probably done 'as far as possible in the same condition as it was before', which was the wish of the landdrost and his heemraden. Although it was stipulated

There is considerable detail to be found in the plasterwork of many Stellenbosch buildings.

Top left The 'all-seeing eye of God' admonishes one from the front gable of La Gratitude in Dorp Street.

Centre left The palm tree is the emblem of both the Village Museum and the Stellenbosch Dutch Reformed Church. This one adorns the façade of Grosvenor House.

Bottom left This most appropriate detail occurs on a wall on the road to Jonkershoek.

Right The façade of 149 Dorp Street is unusual in that, when the front door was moved from the central position because of internal changes, a second door was not added to restore the original symmetry.

A glorious view of Stellenbosch from the Devon Valley road. Blue dams mirror a clear sky, and a rounded hillock, geometrically patterned by farming activities, hides a part of Simon van der Stel's town.

that the rebuilt houses should have 'bricked flat roofs' instead of the inflammable thatch, it seems that this regulation was not closely adhered to.

There was a flutter of a different sort in November 1740 during the time of Hendrik Swellengrebel, first Cape-born governor, when Frans Diederik Muller announced that he had discovered a rich source of silver on Simonsberg. Staid Company officials were particularly excited but they should have known better; perhaps they had forgotten earlier experiences of Cape silver-mining. During Simon van der Stel's governorship so-called experts happily defrauded the Company by pretending to extend a flooded shaft on the farm Witteboomen on the Cape Peninsula until they were found out by a master miner, coincidentally named Muller. A similar episode further south on the Peninsula is still recalled by its name – Silvermine. Now it was the turn of Stellenbosch.

The Company, it is true, was unwilling to risk its own capital in the venture but permission was given for the formation of a private mining company on condition that 15 per cent of the value of useful minerals found was to be paid to the Lords Seventeen. The formation of a company of this kind was a first for both Stellenbosch and South Africa but, sad to say, neither the principal shareholder – one of the church elders named Olof de Wet – nor the church nor the Lords Seventeen received any return whatever. Mining activity on the slopes of Simonsberg went on for more than five years with Frans Muller and his workmen keeping up an encouraging front. When the shareholders became inquisitive, Muller assured them that not only would his mines yield silver but also copper and gold. Greed being what it is, these assurances kept the money rolling in but there came a day when even the trusting burghers of Stellenbosch had had enough. In 1748 ore samples were sent to Holland, which is what one would have expected to have been done in the first place. The report that came back confirmed that the shareholders had been duped – the 'ore' contained no mineral of any value whatever. As for Frans Diederik Muller, he suffered the fate of the fraudulent miners of the previous century and was deported to Batavia.

Naturally, almost nobody at the Cape at that time, or indeed for another 20 years, was English. In the winter of 1795 young Petrus Borcherds, then about nine years of age, recalled walking with his father, the minister of Stellenbosch, in the grounds of the pastorie and hearing, in the evening, the sound of cannon-fire from the direction of False Bay. Next morning, the various detachments of burgher militia were summoned by signal cannon, by fire and by the flying of the red flag – known

as the 'blood flag' – at the Castle. Stellenbosch, too, prepared to do its bit to defend the Cape from the invading British. Five companies of cavalry assembled under their respective flags of green, blue, red, white or yellow, and rode out along the wagon-road to the Cape. Borcherds lists the cavalry company commanders and the number of men each one mustered: they were captains Laubscher (105), Meyburg (156), Van der Byl (144), Hoffman (124) and Cloete (129). Thus Stellenbosch watched as no fewer than 658 of its sons rode to war. It was in deadly earnest, as Borcherds continues: 'The lamentations of wives, mothers, and families were heard from almost every habitation. The pastor did all he could to pacify them, recommending submission to the duties which the government required. The houses in the village were soon crowded with families who had removed from Cape Town, dreading the calamities of war...'

Borcherds told how the martial spirit infected even the boys, about 50 or 60 of whom were enrolled under Commandant Michiel Smuts with Johannes Smuts as lieutenant. They were formed in two companies of infantry, bearing blue and white colours and provided with a drum and a little band. Much to the amusement of the few adults left at home after the rest had gone to war, this little troop of youthful soldiers paraded on the Braak armed with bamboo guns then marched bravely through the village. As a reward for their patriotism, they were invited by Landdrost H L Bletterman to call at the drostdy

where he and his lady – the essence of politeness and civility – provided them with cakes and tea 'in abundance'.

Fortunately, the budding infantrymen were not called on to wield their bamboo guns in anger and, with the surrender of the Dutch garrison at the Cape, hostilities ended and the various corps disbanded.

THE VISITORS

During the rule of the Dutch East India Company and, later, under the British Crown, the Cape held a compelling fascination for many learned and adventurous people in Europe. Botanists were entranced by the profusion of strange and beautiful plants that, within not many decades, were almost as much at home in the conservatories of Europe as they were on the southern African veld. Most of these men of science did their botanizing and dissection in the comfort of their laboratories back home, but some of them braved the long sea voyage to see the wonders of Africa in their natural surroundings.

One such adventurer was Carl Pehr Thunberg, a Swede who, although qualified as a medical doctor, dedicated most of his life to botany. Lacking private means or wealthy sponsors, he served as ship's surgeon on the three-month voyage to the Cape where he arrived in April 1772.

He saw Stellenbosch, having walked there, botanizing en route, from Cape Town. 'Stellenbosch is a village consisting of thirty houses and upwards, with a church; here a landdrost resides... [It] is situated in a narrow valley between high mountains, which are open to the south-west or towards False Bay. It has two streets with oak trees planted in them, and a river running through.'

Lady Anne Barnard, wife of the Cape Colonial Secretary and 'first lady' of the colony in the absence of the governor's wife, describes a visit made in November 1797 to 'Stillingbosch'. She also wrote it as 'Stellingbosh' but, by the end of her visit, had managed to get the spelling correct. Lady Anne's powers of observation and almost mischievous sense of humour somehow survive her erratic spelling and punctuation. She wrote that the party went over the Cape Flats by way of 'the Koyle' – her interpretation of 'De Kuylen', a farm in the vicinity of present-day Kuils River which had become the recognized half-way house between Cape Town and Stellenbosch. The landdrost to whom she refers was Rijno van der Riet, a Cape-born official who successively served the Dutch East India Company, the British during their first occupation of the Cape, the Batavian republican administration and the British again when they returned, in 1806, to occupy the Cape permanently.

Left *A family coat of arms seen on the road to Jonkershoek bears, appropriately, a bunch of grapes.*

Right *Like the old Kruithuis, the Ou Hoofgebou, or Old Main Building of the University of Stellenbosch, is one of the town's truly distinctive structures. It dates from 1879.*

'The Landrost of Stillingbosh had pressed us to come to his house,' wrote Lady Anne. 'He had two pretty daughters and a good humoured wife, but as the Ladys could neither Spraken English nor french, and as we have never before found any necessity of speaking dutch consequently are too ignorant of it, I preferred accepting of the empty house of the Fiscals in the same village where I thought we should be more at liberty, and give less trouble; consenting however to dine with them every day and to accept of their carriage and Horses together with the most illustrious Coachman of the old governor Zluiskin [Abraham Josias Sluysken, last governor under the Dutch East India Company] now theirs, to drive us to all curious sights near or at a distance – we arrived in time to dinner, and had a plantyfull one, really good, tho in the dutch stile; the Drosty or Landrosts house is more spacious than any other I have been in here, having a sort of second row of rooms behind the first, but the division of every dutch house in the Colony is the same.

A Hall – a square room on each hand & another family eating room behind, with two bed chambers – before his door there is the only two fine oaks I have seen except the others in the village they measure 18 feet round each but the perfection of this place consists in its extreme coolness in the midst of the most sultry weather. It is built in this form – perfectly regular, each street having on each side a row of large oaks which shadow the tops of the Houses keeping them cool and forming a shady avenue between thro which the sun cannot pierce, whichever way one walks one finds an avenue, left or right. Each house has a good garden, Stillingbosh therefore tho there may not be above 100 familys in it covers a good deal of ground, and is so perfectly clean and well built that it appears to be inhabited only by people of small fortunes, but I am told there are many very poor people in it... It seems rather an Asylum for Old age than anything else, and I am told people live longer in it than in any other part of the colony.

'Wine is the chief produce of the lands hereabouts, and a small piece of ground only being necessary to make a great deal of wine the rest of Mother earth lays barren & neglected. 1000 vines make a leagar of wine… the vines are planted in rows and there seems to me to be about 4 feet between vine and vine – but to what an extent the cultivation of wine might be brought here if the farmers were sure of a good market! I never saw the force of prejudice more apparent than in the way our countrymen turn up their foolish noses at the Cape wines, because they are Cape wines…'

Hinrich Lichtenstein was another physician who had turned naturalist. Engaged as family doctor and tutor to the son of General J W Janssens, he arrived at the Cape with his employer, the newly appointed governor, in December 1802 when the Cape was about to be returned to the Batavian Republic. He was to remain until the beginning of 1806. Writing after his return to Europe, Lichtenstein gave rather more space and thought to Stellenbosch than did Thunberg. According to him, 'Stellenbosch is rather a small town than a village. It consists of three long straight streets, running parallel with each other, and several cross streets intersecting them at right angles. The houses are all spacious, and substantially built, though only thatched with straw. Each street resembles an avenue, since, on both sides before the houses, are large shady oaks, which are almost as old as the place itself, and that was built at the very beginning of the former century, though it was wholly burnt down in 1710. A similar accident menaced it but a few months before our arrival. In December 1803 a fire broke out at night…

Above left An open shutter reveals the thickness of the walls of the old armoury, or kruithuis, on the Braak.

Above Mounted on a naval-style carriage, this early bronze breech-loader stands at the kruithuis door.

Right The Western Province has been described as a 'land of oaks and cannon', typified in a scene of fallen leaves and ancient gun barrels behind the kruithuis.

and before the flames could be extinguished, twenty houses were laid in ashes...'

According to Lichtenstein the wine produced in the Stellenbosch district was 'most excellent. Many sorts, when eight or ten years old, are preferred by connoisseurs to Constantia. The houses are large, and conveniently distributed; some are built by no means without taste. In everything there is an appearance of affluence, and if the estates of some may be much encumbered with debts, this would never be suspected in seeing their houses and tables. For the rest, the people collectively have all a certain degree of education and cultivation, and some may justly be considered as among the most truly estimable in the whole colony'.

Another writer who commented on Stellenbosch was a young man named John Thomas Pocock who kept a diary from the age of 12 until his death 50 years later. As the apprentice to a Cape Town physician, one of his duties was to go about the countryside delivering accounts. The doctor, it seems, had some slow-paying patients in Stellenbosch in 1834. 'Stellenbosch is a very pretty town,' wrote Pocock; 'it is composed of seven or eight streets laid out with great regularity... each of which has two rows of lofty trees... there is a fine shady walk to the right of the church... and a small stream of clear water running down towards the town. I crossed the bridge and walked up towards the berg... by the side of a hedge of Quince trees laden with fruit, this walk delighted my vivid fancy, all was silent, natural, green...'

Margaret Stewart, whose marriage to astronomer Sir John Herschel was described as a 'union of unclouded happiness', saw Stellenbosch within a month of young Pocock and his account book. 'Stellenbosch is a very old Dutch Town,' commented Lady Herschel. 'An avenue of oaks runs along the street, through which you can scarcely perceive a house at all – & as there does not seem to be any shop except a druggist's, the town has more the appearance of a "City of the Dead" than might be expected from its size. But it makes a beautiful picture of still life with its dazzling white houses, the rich green trees, & those glorious mountains which rise just above it... Our Innkeeper Mr Konisberg was almost the only man who could speak English – the Government School even, is conducted in Dutch...' Her innkeeper was not Mr 'Konisberg' at all, but David Kinneburgh, sheriff of Stellenbosch. He had bought the former parsonage of Het Stellenbossche Medewerkend Zendinggenootschap in Dorp Street in 1824 and ran it as a guest house. Sir John Herschel, during their visit, sat down with his camera lucida, a simple optical instrument to assist in accurate draw-ing, and recorded a street scene. There are the oaks in bounteous leaf; there are gables and fluted parapets and, in the street, an ox-wagon laden with huge casks has come to a halt. Meticulous Sir John even recorded the pendent nests of weaver birds and a fat gentleman chatting on a street corner. (It is interesting to note that when the artist Thomas Bowler painted a Stellenbosch street scene in 1867 he also included a wine wagon with oxen apparently taking their ease. The pace of life that both pictures convey is distinctly less than frantic.)

By 1851 John Rose, a civil servant of Cape Town, was able to travel to Stellenbosch in some style by the regular omnibus service, a journey that took three and a half hours. But better things were in store. In May 1862 John Rose was able to record in his diary that he 'started for Stellenbosch by train on Saturday at 1.20 p.m. and arrived at that village at 3 p.m. Spent Sunday there, and returned to town this morning at 9.40 a.m. having left Stellenbosch at 8 a.m. It is now quite delightful to run down by rail, instead of the dusty omnibuses'.

A few months later Rose was able to condense his visits to Stellenbosch into a single day, thanks to the speed of the new railway. 'Took Ellen [his sister] on her first visit to Stellenbosch,' he wrote. 'We left town at 8 a.m. and returned to town by the 6 p.m. train, having enjoyed a delightful day.'

Stellenbosch entered the railway age on 18 March 1862 when the gleaming locomotive, *Sir George Grey*, steamed into the town. The original plan had been for a line from Cape Town to Wellington via Paarl with branch lines leading to Stellenbosch, Malmesbury and Wynberg. In the end, the line approved by the Colonial Government, and the route that was eventually constructed, was one that ran from Cape Town through Stellenbosch and Paarl to Wellington.

Some 40 years later, in 1907, the Cape Government Railways published a guidebook called *Cape Colony To-Day*. If some of the facts are less than accurate (there is a picture of the Theological Seminary captioned 'Old Dutch House', for instance), the writer's enthusiasm ought to ensure him forgiveness. 'At the beginning of civilization in the Cape,' he informs the reader, 'its domestic, social and political affairs were arranged and directed in the forum of Van der Stel. The world is familiar with the origin of the place and its name. But briefly let us say that Commandant Van der Stel and his good wife Mary, whose maiden name was Bosch, in the year 1681 gave their combined names to the town.' This is an interesting piece of misinformation, no doubt suggested by the origins of the names of Swellendam and Graaff-Reinet, in which those of husbands and wives were indeed combined.

The railway enthusiast continues: 'This excellent couple, besides laying a goodly number of foundation stones (Where, one wonders again, did he find his information?), planted avenues with rows of oak trees, one at least of which lives to-day, and stately scions of the old stock grace the town... Many other things are so reminiscent of the eighteenth century that after a few hours' sojourn one seems to be meeting and living with the people of a bye-gone and forgotten age, half ancient and half modern in their ideas and ideals...'

The writer of the guidebook had this to say about Stellenbosch as an educational centre: 'Many young Dutchmen and Dutchwomen from all parts of the Colony are educated here. Indeed, to be well educated is, in Stellenbosch elite opinion, the first and foremost duty of the man of the world... The students in residence attend the different colleges in pursuit of degrees and diplomas, and domestic affairs at the hostel are consistently congenial, for added to the "home comforts" is a technical school of cookery, an instructional laundry, and a dress-making school. Music, debates, walks and games completely fill up the recreation... It will occasion no surprise, therefore, to find that it is to this ancient town that many well-to-do farmers of the faraway veld proudly send their sons and daughters for collegiate training. They emerge educationally well equipped, bearing with them the Stellenbosch impress, as ineffaceable as the memories of boyhood always are.' The students were not called Maties then, but the pride in being of Stellenbosch is clearly of ancient origin.

Although Stellenbosch did not become too directly involved in inter-continental shipping, the Union-Castle Mail Steamship Company very properly included a description of its history and some of its delights in their 1913 edition of *The Guide to South and East Africa for the use of Tourists, Sportsmen, Invalids and Settlers*. This annual volume, in its heyday, was almost an official guidebook – even if it did get the facts wrong here and there. This is what its compilers (after repeating the bit about Commandant van der Stel and his wife, the former Miss Bosch) had to say about Stellenbosch: 'In the centre of the town, as in most others planned by the Dutch, is a large grass-grown square or common, known as the Braak, which, in the early days of the village, was the scene of an annual fair of considerable importance. The most noticeable feature of the town is the number of magnificent oak avenues... Under the leafy arcades the stillness of the cloisters reigns during the heat of the day and a South African Rip Van Winkle might awake, after a lengthy nap, without finding many modern innovations to surprise him...

'The principal buildings are the Victoria College, an extensive establishment with a Grecian façade; the Boys' High School, the Bloemhof and Rhenish Girls' Schools, the Theological Seminary of the Dutch Church, the Dutch, English, Rhenish and Wesleyan Churches and the handsome Y.M.C.A. building. There is a small library. Stellenbosch has always been an important educational centre and its schools and colleges rank among the first in South Africa.'

To the modern visitor, Stellenbosch appears to boast the normal developments of any progressive town while retaining much of its old-world charm and appeal. Restaurants and eating-places abound, some with the atmosphere of the Continental sidewalk café and almost all patronized by students who seem to grow younger each year. Streetside furrows flash with running water and do not appear the hazard they have been declared in so many other towns that have bricked them over. Stellenbosch, one concludes, has been fortunate in that its people have found it, and worked to preserve it.

Small, casement windows reflect the blue Stellenbosch sky.

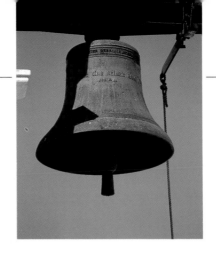

*'...him that bringeth good tidings, that publisheth
peace, that bringeth good tidings of good...'*

'THE FACE OF GOD...'

ACCORDING to the Book of Genesis (Chapter 32), Jacob gave the name of Peniel to the place where, alone, he wrestled with God, 'for I have seen God face to face, and my life is preserved'. For churchmen in early Stellenbosch, in trying to show to their often recalcitrant congregations the face of God, there was also some wrestling to be done.

To start with, there seems to have been some apathy that greatly annoyed Commander Simon van der Stel who, having instructed that a drostdy and godshuis, or place of worship, be built, arrived a few months later and found that almost nothing had been done. On this occasion, in 1686, he brought with him the Reverend Johannes Overneij who had been persuaded to stay at the Cape while on his way to the East some eight years earlier. He loved the place and during the period of his pastoral administration was the only ordained minister of the church resident in the entire colony. Notwithstanding the absence of a church, Overneij duly held a service, with sermon, in the house of one of the burghers on Sunday 13 October. His choice of text seems to suggest a man who loved his God and the lovely countryside in which he found himself – and

in which he founded a new congregation. It is from Isaiah 52: 7 and reads, 'How beautiful upon the mountain are the feet of him that bringeth good tidings, that publisheth peace; that bringeth good tidings of good, that publisheth salvation; that saith unto Zion, Thy God reigneth!' Symbolic of the new inland colony and its potential for growth was the baptism of three infants at the same service.

Soon after the visit a real beginning was made with building the church, a foundation stone being laid not to the glory of God but 'in honour of the Founder of the Colony' – that is, Simon van der Stel himself. This, at any rate, is the interpretation placed upon a short letter written by Van der Stel to Douwe Steyn (or Stein), the mason in charge, though it is just possible that when Van der Stel wrote 'den Stigter van die Colonie' he referred not to himself but to Almighty God as its spiritual founder. However, the first stone was duly laid, apparently without ceremony or even the attendance of any high official or ordained minister. It was the ambition of Overneij to preach and administer Holy Communion in this little building – the first to be erected in South Africa as a permanent church. It was

*Left St Mary's Anglican Church on the Braak is
a charming blend of styles and periods.*

*Above The great bell of the Rhenish Church
has summoned many generations of worshippers.*

Below *Reminders of mortality are the skull and crossed bones, and the winged hourglass. This is to be found in the grounds of the Moederkerk.*

Right *The Rhenish Mission Church, at the southern edge of the Braak, is among the oldest – and most beautiful – of the country's churches.*

completed on 4 May 1687 but on the same day the sad news reached Stellenbosch that the Reverend Johannes Overneij had died at his home in the Table Valley the night before.

The Cape settlement was once again without a clergyman, although fortunately not for long for only a month later the Reverend Johannes van Andel arrived. Like Overneij, he had been on his way to the East but was requested to stay, which he did for some 18 months. And so, on 19 October 1687, in the presence of the commander, Van Andel consecrated the church of Stellenbosch, choosing as his text Numbers 6: 22-27, which is God's blessing on the children of Israel. The church appears clearly in a drawing by E V de Stade made in February 1710 as a rectangular building with a fairly high and steeply pitched thatched roof. It occupies a block of land bordered in part by what seems to be a low-growing hedge and at one end, slightly off-centre – and perhaps even detached – is a bell tower. The church did not long survive its depiction on paper for it was destroyed in the disastrous fire that swept the little colony in December that year.

The first permanent minister at Stellenbosch was the Reverend Hercules van Loon who, in a fit of despair and depression, slit his own throat in 1704, only four years after his arrival. To fill the position so sadly and shockingly vacated, the Reverend Henricus Beck of Drakenstein was appointed to Stellenbosch without being relieved of his other parish. Beck, married to the daughter of an official who sided with unpopular Governor Wilhem Adriaen van der Stel, was regarded with some suspicion, not least by Adam Tas, a deacon of the church. In Tas's diary, the clergyman appears as 'the so-called preacher Bek' – the misspelling, a crude word for 'mouth', being deliberate. As the relationship soured yet further, the unfortunate minister became 'Father Bek' and even, like Anglican Bishop Gray to his critics in the 19th century, 'the Pope'. While it may well be impossible to please all people all of the time, poor Beck seemed to please scarcely anyone.

It was during Beck's period of service that the new church was built, even though more than 10 years passed between the destruction of the first building and the inauguration of the second. To help swell the church funds, Beck resorted to a method contentious even in the South Africa of the 1990s – he ran a lottery. While this unorthodox practice did bring in some money, it brought greater troubles in its wake, with Beck being accused of not handing out prizes and even, when he had left Stellenbosch, of retaining items of church silver.

Bearing in mind that the old church was destroyed by fire during a fierce south-easterly gale, it was resolved to erect the

new building upwind of the settled area of the village, where it would be protected should ever a fire start in one of the houses or other buildings. On that site stands the present Moederkerk which contains within it some of the fabric of the second church which was, in plan, a cross with arms of equal length. (The worn foundations of the original church are still to be seen beneath the building in Church Street known as D'Ouwe Werf.) An anonymous painting of 1757 shows the second church within its walled grounds, the arm facing Church Street bearing a restrained Baroque gable with, close by, a simple, free-standing little bell tower. What the painting does not show is the wonderful range of stained-glass windows installed in 1725. These, which would have been an incomparable aid to a genealogist or heraldry enthusiast and a delight to any eye, depicted in full colour the family crests or attainments of many of the early Stellenbosch families. Today, only two of these crests survive, and these almost by accident.

It is clear from correspondence that the church was too small for its congregation by 1791 when Philippus Mijburgh of Meerlust offered to pay for extensions. Mijburgh was not merely wealthy but downright frank. He was sick and tired of not being able to find a place to sit in the church, he said, and added that if the situation continued he would consider either bringing his own chair or finding some less-crowded place of worship to attend. Unaccountably, the church council did not avail itself of Mijburgh's offer and we are told that, thereafter, he became only a very irregular churchgoer. In fact, it was only in 1807 that the church was enlarged by an extension of the east wing to create a vestry. Up to this time the floor had been simply of earth and burials within the building were fairly commonplace, although at least one vault outside it survives from this early period. However, 1807 saw another improvement – the laying of a floor of tiles made by one of the church deacons and supplied by him at little more than cost price. Once this new floor was laid, burials inside the church were no longer practicable and more spaces for vaults along the ring wall were made available, The vaults are well worth a close inspection, some for their stories of lives and deaths, some for their macabre carvings. Look in the church grounds, too, for the olive tree from the Garden of Gethsemane.

Back inside the church, galleries had been introduced to provide additional seating for a growing congregation, but the problem of sufficient space was not solved – and then, only temporarily – until 1814, when the remaining three wings were enlarged. This meant the loss of the Baroque gable which was replaced with one of a pattern then currently in style and itself

Left The bold colours of this stained-glass window, and of several others, are to be seen in the Moederkerk, or Mother Church, of the Dutch Reformed Church (right).

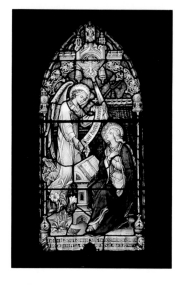

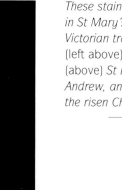

These stained-glass windows in St Mary's Church typify the Victorian tradition. They depict (left above) the Annunciation, (above) St Peter and St Andrew, and (left below) the risen Christ.

Left *The Rhenish parsonage and, indeed, the entire Rhenish complex, is one of the jewels of early Cape architecture, with a harmony of styles that includes classic Cape Dutch, unadorned Victorian and even a touch of Renaissance.*

Above *The National Monuments Council emblem is mounted above the bronze plaque that tells, in brief, the story of the Rhenish Mission Church building.*

destined to disappear in the great rebuilding by Carl Otto Hager in the 1860s. It was during this conversion to Hager's beloved Gothic style that almost all the stained-glass windows were lost. It seems incredible that in the excitement of gaining a 'new' church, apparently no thought whatever was given to retaining what might have been worthwhile of the old, other than some basic wall structures. It was a visitor to the site in 1862 who found and preserved two sections of glass bearing arms related to his own family ancestors, the Morkels, which today are cherished as treasures of the Village Museum.

Hager's plan for the church building, completed in 1863, was carried out by the contractor James Jardine of Worcester, but certainly not without considerable hard feeling on both sides. The pulpit, ascended by a flight of 11 extremely steep steps, is a marvellous exposition of the Gothic style, with the sounding board surmounted by what appears to be a miniature medieval cathedral and all of it exquisitely carved of wood to the design of Carl Otto Hager. Only 10 years earlier, the church council had decided to dispense with the old pulpit built and donated by the Albertyn family in 1721, possibly because they now felt it to be insufficiently ornate. Simon Pieter Londt, a cabinet-maker of Cape Town, was duly engaged to replace it with one that was more elaborate. This second pulpit reveals that Londt, although referred to as a 'cabinet-maker', was clearly a master carver in the tradition of Anton Anreith. However, Londt's pulpit and its *voorleser's* lectern were felt to be not in harmony with Hager's Gothic lines and so were offered to the missionaries of the nearby Rhenish Church who, recognizing a work of art when they saw one, promptly accepted the gift. And so the Londt pulpit, in all its magnificence, is still to be seen in the Rhenish Church on the Braak.

When this mission church was inaugurated in 1823, the Reverend Meent Borcherds chose as his text the first verse of Psalm 84 – 'How lovely are Thy dwellings, O Lord of Hosts' – words that must seem most appropriate to anyone stirred by the serenity of classical ecclesiastical architecture. At that time only that portion of the church lying parallel to the nearest edge of the Braak had been built. It included a gable thought to have been a copy of the one which had decorated the front of the Moederkerk since its 1814 enlargement. The site soon developed as the needs of a growing congregation demanded more space. In fact, in its original form, the Rhenish Church lasted no more than 14 years and though the missionaries must have been gratified at this evidence of labour rewarded, their pleasure must have been somewhat tempered by the realization that money would be needed to pay for the extensions.

There was no lottery this time: money was donated by the local missionary society and more was collected in Cape Town. Most heart-warming of all was the response to an appeal by the Reverend Paulus Daniel Lückhoff for women of the congregation to donate personal items of gold, silver or jewellery. By no means well-to-do, these good women – mindful of the biblical injunction not to lay up for themselves treasure on earth – duly gave what they had. And that what they had was not a great deal is shown by the fact that the value raised was no more than 100 rix dollars. Not to be shamed by their womenfolk, the men of the congregation collected an almost identical sum and legend has it that a further contribution was their willing labour in erecting the extension, completed in 1840 with yet another gracious but different gable. The enterprise had originally been under the direction of the Stellenbosch Missionary Society but control had transferred to the Rhenish Missionary Society in 1829.

The 'new' extension of the Rhenish Mission Church looks out over the Braak on which the only building is the Anglican church of St Mary. For much of the 19th century, Anglicans at the Cape had to rely on the unfailing generosity of the Dutch Reformed Church councils in allowing them to hold services in their churches. However, with the arrival of the first Bishop of Cape Town, Robert Gray, in 1848, a programme of church-building was set in motion. In the year of his arrival, Gray visited Stellenbosch during a lengthy circuit of his immense diocese, which included most of the present South Africa. His wife, Sophy, was an enthusiastic draughtswoman and adaptor of church plans, of which she had brought a great number to her new home. At that time, clergy received their salary, or stipend, from the Colonial Government. This unhealthy situation, which was to continue for several decades until the passing of the Voluntary Bill, meant that government had a disproportionately large say in the running of church affairs. However, it did mean that a clergyman could be appointed to Stellenbosch, and this was the Reverend Frederick Carlyon who took up his post in 1850. One of his secular talents was collecting funds for worthy causes, and it was not long before he had a church building.

In its original form, as a simple rectangle to hold about 80 people, St Mary's Church was consecrated by the bishop in October 1854, just a few days after Simon van der Stel's birthdate and at a time when the Braak was named Adderley Square. Alterations and additions were made several times, one said to have been under the supervision and to the plan of Herbert Baker. Carlyon's successor, the Reverend Jacob Legg, must have been an enterprising man and it is worth noting that he experimented with exporting fruit to Covent Garden Market in London. For his first attempt, in 1888, he used refrigerated space in the liner *Grantully Castle*. At best, his results in this venture could be described as mixed, but his efforts on behalf of his church were more successful. The official guide to St Mary's Church states that 'the church as it stands today, is a memorial to his untiring efforts'. The amount of input by Sophy Gray regarding the design is unsure. Most of 'her' little churches in Cape country towns are of dressed stone, but several have the plastered, whitewashed finish of St Mary's.

Another church building of some age and interest no longer performs its original function. This is the old Lutheran Evangelical Church building in Dorp Street, now an art gallery of the University of Stellenbosch. Many Dutch East India Company officials, especially soldiers, were of German origin and of the Lutheran faith, but were forbidden by Company law to hold any form of public service until late in the 18th century. By the mid 19th century there was a sizeable community of Lutherans in Stellenbosch and in 1851 a collection was made for the purpose of building a church. Approached for a donation, Carl Otto Hager, who was going through one of his financially shaky spells, offered to draw the plans in lieu of a cash contribution. If he really did play only a part in designing St Mary's Cathedral in Cape Town (as is claimed), then the little Lutheran Church may have been his first solo effort at planning a church.

Predictably, Hager drew a design in the Gothic Revival style of which he was such a dedicated proponent; this was happily accepted and the church was inaugurated in 1854. When, as all Stellenbosch churches seem to do, it became too small, there was no space on the site for enlargements and so a new church was built. The original one then became a shop, complete with display windows, but fortunately, when it was already more than 100 years old, it was restored and presented to the University.

The river that flows through Stellenbosch, the Eerste River, reaches the sea some 15 km away shortly after flowing through the farm Zandvliet. Now, across town from Dorp Street – at the corner of Andringa and Banhoek roads – there is a strong link with Zandvliet and an expression of the faith of Islam. It was in 1694 that Sheik Yussuf, of Macassar in Indonesia, was brought as a political prisoner to the Cape and eventually settled, with his retinue, on the farm Zandvliet. The mere presence in the colony of Sheik Yussuf, a learned and pious man, is thought to have helped many Muslims – most of them slaves – to keep their faith under trying conditions. The Banhoek Road mosque of 1897 has a minaret, as do almost all mosques, but perhaps it is because this is Stellenbosch that it also has a gable.

There are other religions in Stellenbosch, and other houses of prayer. Our scrutiny has fallen only upon some of the older ones; in these gracious buildings, through many generations, people have expressed an understanding of those lovely words: 'how beautiful upon the mountain are the feet of him that bringeth good tidings…'

Churchgoers greet one another beneath the Moederkerk's soaring spire.

*'Many are the bricks in that building that
were made under my eye…'*

THE TOWN OF OAKS

IT WAS SIMON VAN DER STEL who encouraged the planting of trees 'both indigenous and from the fatherland', but it was Commissioner Hendrik van Reede tot Drakestein who gave it as his authoritative view that oaks would be the most suitable. A mere commander did not argue with a commissioner-general of the Honourable East India Company, and so, although not entirely at home in a climate so mild compared to that of their native Europe, oaks were planted, took root and grew.

Oaks lined the streets when Stellenbosch was no more than a few blocks bounded by the tracks that are now Dorp and Plein, Drostdy and Bird streets. Herein lies the town's historical nucleus, with a few more distant features such as the Braak and farms that, once on the outskirts of town, are now well within its embrace. Perhaps Dorp Street, with its mellowness of oaks and gables, is the most evocative of the early days when this was the wagon-road to the Cape. Now it contains the largest number and, perhaps, the greatest variety of old or interesting buildings in town. And to see them as they deserve to be seen, you must leave your wagon and take a slow walk under the oaks.

Let's start towards the west end of Dorp Street at its intersection with Strand Road. We shall be strolling east, so the right-hand side of the road will be the south side and the left, the north. Look back a moment, west, in the direction of Adam Tas Street, at the double-storeyed Edwardian building on the north side. This handsome pile is Oude Rozenhof, built as the National Hotel to take advantage of the weekend streams of sightseers disembarking from the Cape Town train at nearby Bosman's Crossing siding. It seemed a good idea at the time but, unaccountably, the proprietors failed to ensure that they would be able to obtain the necessary liquor licence. They were not, and the custom that their liquorless hotel attracted was minimal. A temperance hotel in the heart of the winelands was something of a joke and so it became for some years a boarding house for young ladies and was particularly favoured by 'parlour boarders'.

On the right, between Strand Road and Old Strand Road, is a little cluster of classic Cape Dutch buildings now housing a wine museum and art gallery. Once the homestead of Klein Libertas, also known as Libertas Parva, it was formerly a portion of Oude Libertas, the

Left *A plain Georgian façade rubs shoulders
with Cape Dutch – without any serious visual clash.*

Above *Wisteria trails over an old wall in Herte Street.*

farm belonging to Adam Tas. This part of town, on the south side of Dorp Street between Strand Road and Piet Retief Street, is known as Krigeville after the Krige family, one of whom was Jacob Daniel Krige who married Susanna Schabort. With their 11 children, including lively Sybella, they occupied Libertas Parva at a time when one of Mrs Ackermann's boarders – at 50 Dorp Street, just across the road – was an earnest young student from Riebeeck West named Jan Smuts. Somewhere here they met, were properly introduced in the manner of the day and, in 1897, married in a front room of the Krige homestead. This was built around 1800 by Lambertus Fick, one of the town's fire-wardens, but it is thought that the lovely gables were added some 20 years later. And across the road, Number 50 has been restored to what it is believed to have been in the days of its glory. Certainly, in the days when Mrs Ackermann ran her boarding house it had no gable and sported a roof of corrugated iron in place of thatch. With moulded parapet and enclosed portico, Number 48, adjoining, resembles the Georgian style.

The original H-shaped floor plan of Libertas Parva represented the ultimate development of designs that followed the outlines of letters of the alphabet. The final layout, with one wing longer than the other, no longer qualifies as a letter of the alphabet, but it is possible to see how the plans evolved. The earliest houses, such as Schreuderhuis, now part of the Village Museum, were simply a row of two or three rooms along the street frontage. This was the letter I, modified to L by the backwards extension of a room at one end. Extensions at both ends produced the U-plan, the space between the wings forming a courtyard. The T-shaped design was created by building the extension or 'tail' from the middle of the I instead of from the end, a plan that had the advantage of having the voorkamer, or livingroom, at the centre. Another variation was the letter F developed from the L-plan by building an additional tail from the centre.

THE SILVER THREAD

Make a short detour down Old Strand Road and pause a moment on the bridge to look down on the Eerste River. It was these waters, rising in the mountains above the town and flowing like a silver thread through the lovely valley of Jonkershoek, that prompted Commander Simon van der Stel to call into being the new colony of Stellenbosch. Once covered with indigenous woodland, the upper mountain slopes today are a forestry reserve where, among sighing pines, wary picnickers debate whether the mushrooms are edible or otherwise.

One of the first farms downstream is Old Nectar, whose stately gable, occupying one third of the frontage of the house, can be seen above the foliage from the Jonkershoek road. When it was owned by the free black, Jan of Ceylon, the place took on its owner's nickname, which was Jan Lui. His neighbour, where the river widens, was another free black, Louis of Bengal who owned Klein Gustrow, the farm once known as Leef-op-Hoop. Down the valley the river courses past Lanzerac, now a hotel on the edge of Stellenbosch town in the suburb called Mostertsdrift. Close by at the weir, sluice gates divert a part of the flow into the millstream, which for many years was an important industrial artery of the town. Here too, when it was a shady lane beside the stream, was Lovers' Walk, a promenade familiar to generations of students.

Below the town the river flows through Doornbosch, granted to Jacob Aartsz Brouwer in 1692 and just over the way from Libertas, once the farm of diarist and rebel Adam Tas. The homestead, though, dates from long after his ownership. An earlier owner of Libertas, Hans Jurgen Grimpe, whose widow Tas was to marry, himself paid for the erection over the Eerste River of 'a large and stately bridge for the common benefit...'

After Libertas the river passes Vredenburg and Vlottenburg and the many-gabled buildings of Spier probably dating from 1767 and shortly thereafter. A narrow arch where a slave bell was hung stands almost on the river bank here. Downstream are the old farms of Welmoed and Klein Welmoed and then the river runs past magnificent Meerlust, property of the Mijburgh family since 1757. This was the domain of Philip Mijburgh who, when British forces occupied the Cape for the second time in 1806, refused to take the oath of loyalty to the new regime. His punishment was to have a troop of heavy dragoons quartered on his farm but to the shrewd Mijburgh, this presented no hardship and he soon won the dragoons over with his kindness and hospitality. They showed their gratitude by building him a stable, and by making numerous items of furniture for the house. In the end, neighbours complained that, instead of punishing a malcontent, the authorities had merely presented Mijburgh with a squad of free labourers. The Acting-Governor eventually saw the point and the dragoons, to their great regret, were withdrawn to barracks in Cape Town. (Meerlust, with its wonderfully preserved buildings which include a most decorative dovecote, is not open to the public.)

The road to the east once crossed the Eerste River, first by a drift and later by a bridge of teak laid on stone pillars, about a kilometre north of Meerlust. Vergenoegd, near the little village of Faure, is another famous and beautiful farm on the

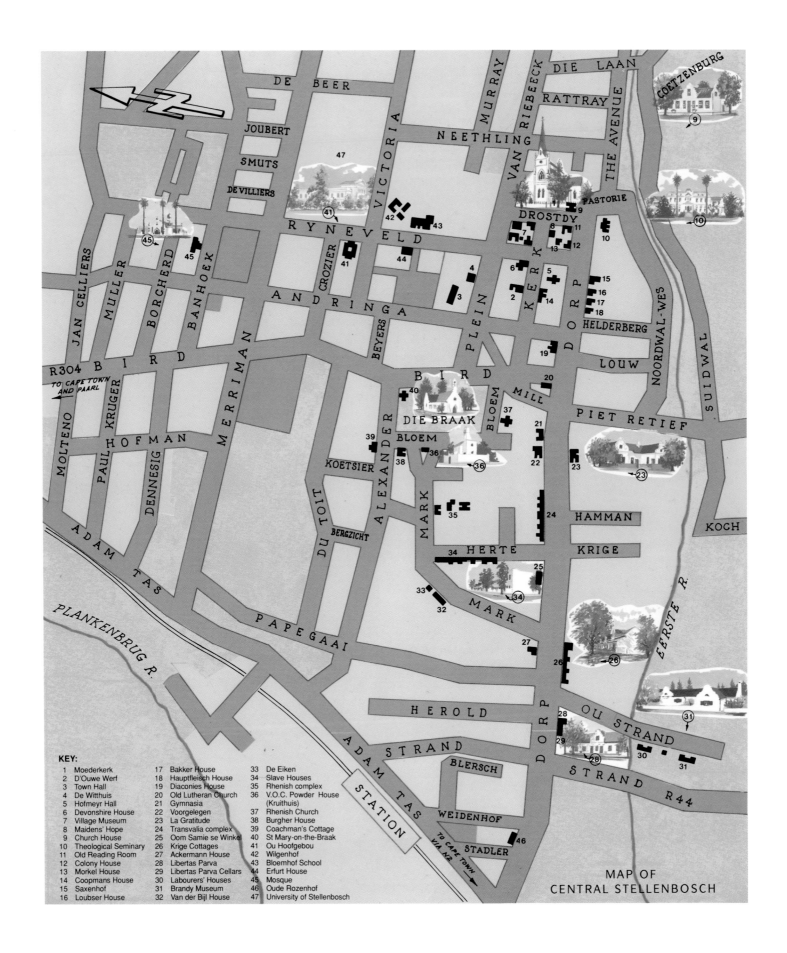

DE BEER

JOUBERT

SMUTS

DE VILLIERS

COETZENBURG

9

NEETHLING

DIE LAAN

RATTRAY

MURRAY

VAN RIEBEECK

THE AVENUE

47

RYNEVELD

VICTORIA

41

42 43

DROSTDY

PASTORIE

9

7 8 11

13 12

10

CROZIER

41

44

ANDRINGA

4

6

5

3

2

14

KERK

PLEIN

DORP

15

16

17

18

HELDERBERG

JAN CELLIERS

MULLER

BORCHERD

BANHOEK

45

45

BEYERS

19

DORP

LOUW

10

R304

BIRD

TO CAPE TOWN
AND PAARL

MERRIMAN

PAUL KRUGER

HOFMAN

DENNESIG

MOLTENO

BIRD

20

MILL

PIET RETIEF

NOORDWAL-WES

SUIDWAL

KOCH

DU TOIT

BERGZICHT

KOETSIER

ALEXANDER

40

DIE BRAAK

BLOEM

39

38

36

37

BLOEM

36

21

22

23

23

ADAM TAS

PAPEGAAI

MARK

35

34

HERTE

24

HAMMAN

KRIGE

25

34

33

32

27

MARK

26

26

ADAM TAS

PLANKENBRUG R.

HEROLD

STRAND

DORP

28

OU STRAND

29

STATION

BLERSCH

WEIDENHOF

STADLER

31

30

31

STRAND R44

EERSTE R.

KEY:

1 Moederkerk	17 Bakker House	33 De Eiken
2 D'Ouwe Werf	18 Hauptfleisch House	34 Slave Houses
3 Town Hall	19 Diaconies House	35 Rhenish complex
4 De Witthuis	20 Old Lutheran Church	36 V.O.C. Powder House
5 Hofmeyr Hall	21 Gymnasia	(Kruithuis)
6 Devonshire House	22 Voorgelegen	37 Rhenish Church
7 Village Museum	23 La Gratitude	38 Burgher House
8 Maidens' Hope	24 Transvalia complex	39 Coachman's Cottage
9 Church House	25 Oom Samie se Winkel	40 St Mary-on-the-Braak
10 Theological Seminary	26 Krige Cottages	41 Ou Hoofgebou
11 Old Reading Room	27 Ackermann House	42 Wilgenhof
12 Colony House	28 Libertas Parva	43 Bloemhof School
13 Morkel House	29 Libertas Parva Cellars	44 Erfurt House
14 Coopmans House	30 Labourers' Houses	45 Mosque
15 Saxenhof	31 Brandy Museum	46 Oude Rozenhof
16 Loubser House	32 Van der Bijl House	47 University of Stellenbosch

MAP OF
CENTRAL STELLENBOSCH

river. Last farm of all is Zandvliet, granted in 1699 to the Reverend Petrus Kalden who, following complaints from his congregation that he spent more time on farming matters than he did on church affairs, was recalled to Holland. On Zandvliet the Eerste River is joined by the Kuils River – the river of pools – and flows close to the kramat or shrine erected over the burial place of Sheik Yussuf, that religious nobleman and exile, whose tomb erected here in 1699 has become the most important Islamic shrine in South Africa. And close by, the Eerste River, the river of Stellenbosch, that has seen men come and go, flows quiet to the sea.

WAGON-ROAD TO THE CAPE

Back in Stellenbosch, just beyond the bridge over the river, there is a restaurant where you can dine out under the oaks and, further on, a brandy museum occupying cottages said to have been designed by Herbert Baker for labourers on the farm Vredenburg when it was owned by his friend and mentor Cecil Rhodes. Baker was enchanted by the Cape Dutch style, and created the variation on it that became known as Cape Dutch Revival. With the arrival of corrugated iron as a more practical roofing material than thatch, many gables had been clipped or shorn of their curves so that the iron sheets could be more easily attached. At the same time, corrugated iron verandas were tacked on to house-fronts, marring their wonderfully symmetrical facades. These and other fashionable practices Baker, supported by Rhodes, rightly saw as an abomination.

On the right-hand side of Dorp Street, beyond the row of little dwellings known as the Krige cottages (some with curi-ously narrow dormer windows like monks' cowls), is Vredelust, once the homestead of the farm Libertas-Oos. There is a grand gable dated 1814 but, sadly, the building was 'modernized' according to the fashion of the early 1900s. This accounts for the heavyweight pillared veranda, although the delicate balus-trade on top of the front wall may be original and lends some light relief. Vredelust was the home of another branch of the Krige family for several generations, and for a while, from the early 1960s, its wine cellar, slightly modified, served as the home theatre for the town's amateur dramatic society.

Over on the left side is the colourful sprawl of Oom Samie se Winkel, named after a former proprietor who ran a general dealer's business here for close to 40 years. In addition to the present general 'winkel', redolent of yesteryear, there is a wine shop and tea garden.

Everyone who has heard of it looks for 'the house with the eye': it is at 95 Dorp Street and is named La Gratitude.

Left *A carriageway gives a glimpse of the back courtyard of a Dorp Street house.*

Below left *This Plein Street gateway is thought to have led to the original burial ground.*

Left *Fine, moulded doors and a fanlight are the welcoming central feature of the classic façade.*

Above *Fluted pilasters lend an air of formality to this doorway to a double-storeyed house in Dorp Street.*

Right *Now the Stellenbosch Hotel, this fine homestead in Dorp Street dates from around the beginning of the 19th century.*

Although never the official parsonage, it was built and occupied by the Reverend Meent Borcherds. Unable to support his family on his small stipend, he purchased a piece of land stretching from the wagon-road to the Eerste River and here he farmed during his spare time. The house was completed around 1798, and the minister's son, Petrus Borchardus Borcherds, mentions his own part in its construction in his reminiscences. 'Many are the bricks in that building,' he writes, 'that were made under my eye, and many were the hours of my superintending the works, whilst my Latin lessons were, nevertheless, expected to be duly finished. By rising at an early hour in the morning and retiring late I managed to accomplish my task so as to give satisfaction... ' At the time he acted as superintendent-of-works, young Petrus was no more than about 12 years old. It is a pity that he does not tell us something of those whom he supervised or how they performed their tasks. Almost certainly they were slaves, but the beautiful gable that they created is passed unremarked.

The eye is in the gable, sculpted in relief and surrounded by radiating lines. (The gable of By-den-weg, off the Polkadraai Road, is very similar in general configuration, and also sports an eye.) La Gratitude's eye is presumed to be 'the all-seeing eye of God' and to denote the Reverend Meent Borcherds's gratitude to God for mercies received. That you may find the same gable and name on the label of a popular and well-established wine is no coincidence. The house was bought early this century by William Charles Winshaw, an American physician who, unaccountably, travelled to South Africa not in any medical capacity but in charge of a consignment of mules for the British army. Liking the country, he stayed on and settled at Stellenbosch where he made grape juice and, eventually, his ideal, which was a pure, natural wine 'for the working man'. Out of this commendable enterprise grew the immense organization known as Stellenbosch Farmers' Winery which, during the 1930s, introduced the dry white wine named La Gratitude. That it is still around after more than 50 years suggests adherence to the founder's precepts.

The ground plan of La Gratitude was originally that of the letter H, with one of the letter's upright lines lying along the Dorp Street frontage. At some time in the past this frontage was extended on either side, and it is possible to see the original, wavy side-gables peeping through the thatch. Additional wings have been added to the rear upright of the H, creating a combined HF. To find out how a typical family spent its day in the years when the cool interior of La Gratitude was new, we turn again to Petrus Borcherds. 'In the morning early

Left *The homestead at Lanzerac, now a hotel, has a stately, ornate beauty, counterpointed by the rugged peaks of the Jonkershoek mountains.*

Below *This is the bright summer garden in Bird Street, at a corner of the Braak.*

Above *Posies of baskets blossom on the stoep of Oom Samie se Winkel as skilled fingers prepare another cluster for display.*

Right *Behind the attractive and symmetrical façade are the premises of an old-style negotie-winkel, once common in rural areas.*

they drink a cup of coffee; about eight o'clock they partook of a moderate breakfast, at which meat appeared, and in some families of French descent light wines; a solid dinner was provided at twelve o'clock; tea and sweetmeats followed at three o'clock; coffee and biscuits or bread and butter came in towards evening, to which were sometimes added on the farms fine fruit in season, such as water and musk melons, grapes &c., served neatly on a little table in front of the house, a repast of which I have often enjoyed. At eight o'clock in the evening supper was served; this usually constituted the family meal. After dinner, however, the early rising in the morning induced a gentle siesta. The mother of the family gave the tone of the household, and in order that nothing might escape observation, she was in the habit of sitting at a small table, with a drawer for her keys, nic-nacs, &c., in the back hall, whence she regulated the duties to be performed by the daughters and female domestics.'

Something to notice about the Cape Dutch house, of which La Gratitude is one of the finest examples, is the symmetry of the front façade. The front door – a double door, in this case – is at the centre under a fanlight. Two half-width windows close to the front door admit light to the voorkamer, and full-width windows are equidistant from the front door and further from it. When it became fashionable to have the front door opening to an entrance passage instead of directly into the family's living-quarters, the half-width windows were done away with.

In their place appeared full-width windows, slightly closer to the front door than they used to be, to light the rooms adjacent to the passage. An additional complication was created when the passage, instead of being central, was made by building a wall down one side of the voorkamer. This, of course, put the front door off-centre and ruined the symmetry of the façade. The aesthetically acceptable solution to this was to build a second front door to balance the first and to place a window between them. There are several houses in Stellenbosch that have this feature and we know that in the 1820s the house of Nicolaas Janssen in Church Street had one front door leading to a schoolroom and the other to the family's living-quarters. A stoep usually runs the full width of the front façade and sometimes has built-in benches in the end-walls.

The gable is probably the most admired and characteristic feature of the Cape Dutch homestead. It is usually the front one that is most decorative, often carrying a date that may signify the year in which the house was built or when the roof was re-thatched. Some have other sculpted decorations which included almost anything from urns to pineapples and the owner sometimes had his own initials entwined with those of his wife set in the centre. Although the earliest, and simplest, front gables existed simply to allow light into the attic, or 'solder', most of the later ones were added primarily for decorative purposes.

Just opposite La Gratitude is Voorgelegen at 116 Dorp Street, one of a row of double-storeyed houses running from Number 100 through to Number 118. An interesting aspect of this row is that every house started out as a single-storeyed and, almost certainly, typical Cape Dutch dwelling. Voorgelegen was built around the same time as La Gratitude – about 1798 – and also to the H-shaped plan. The original symmetry of the façade is still apparent and it is thought that the second storey – with those of most of this row – was added in about 1880, leading to the suspicion that this 'improvement' was prompted, at least in part, by making good the damage caused by the fire of 1875. The double-storeyed Transvalia complex, around 125 Dorp Street, is another example of houses that started out as single-storeys. These were also damaged by fire, this time by the earlier blaze of 1803. The government offered to subsidize repairs but only if flat roofs were built, and this, of course, precluded the use of inflammable thatch. Flat roofs also meant that the walls had to be raised, and so upper floors were added.

Number 120 Dorp Street is a physical landmark in the history of Stellenbosch as a centre of higher learning for this is

Far left *The cool courtyard of Oom Samie se Winkel – with residents.*

Left *Skilled hands at work in the Jean Craig Pottery on the Devon Valley road.*

Right *This is how Oom Samie kept his shop, in the days before impersonal supermarkets.*

the old Stellenbosch Gymnasium. Although it was built specifically to house a school in which scholars would be prepared for entrance to the Theological Seminary, it was actually erected at the expense of Mr J D Joubert, a friend of the Reverend J H Neethling, one of the principal promoters of the scheme. In an act of remarkable generosity, Joubert consented to build the Gymnasium on his property and rent it to the institution. Later he showed still more generosity by reducing the rent by a fairly substantial amount because the Gymnasium was experiencing difficult times. The building was used for its original purpose for only about eight years so it is unlikely that generous Mr Joubert made any money on it – but profit was probably not his intent.

On the left, after passing Mill Street, we reach the old Lutheran Church which serves now as an art gallery. This was probably the first church to be designed solely by German-born Carl Otto Hager who settled in Stellenbosch in 1841. A well-trained portrait painter, Hager found little demand for his painting skills when he arrived from Germany so he turned to architecture while living for a few years in Cape Town. In Stellenbosch, however, he did find work as a portrait painter but, by then, he was too enthusiastic about architecture to abandon his second calling. Another interest that Hager developed was photography and for this purpose he opened a studio which, in addition to his other occupations, kept him very busy indeed. As a member of the recently established Lutheran congregation in Stellenbosch, Hager designed this little church in his favourite neo-Gothic style, free of charge, and it was opened in 1854.

Far left *All children love ice-cream, but only little girls bother to wipe their faces.*

Left *Weavers at their hand looms on Dombeya Farm in Annandale Road.*

Below *These bright skeins of wool were spun by hand on Dombeya Farm.*

Further on at Number 156, there is an elegant carriage-way arch separating a late 19th-century single-storeyed house from one of the double-storeys which surround it. Dating from around 1790 is 155 Dorp Street, known as Bakker House. Meeuwes Janse Bakker was a sailor who, having survived a disastrous shipwreck, dedicated the rest of his life to missionary work. Parts of the adjacent Loubser House, at Number 157, are thought to date from very early in the 18th century. For a while this building was also owned by Bakker who sold it to the Stellenbosch Missionary Society – it had known some rough times before that, according to Adam Tas. In 1705 it was occupied by a cobbler named Jacobus van den Berg who, with his 'ill-natured wife set upon the wife of Christian Martensz, commonly known as Mostert's Mary; the cobbler's wife fetched Mostert's Mary a blow on the head with a pick, which drew blood; the blow caused Mary to fall to the ground, whereupon the cobbler ran to her and trampled the prostrate woman upon the breast, the belly, &c., meanwhile the cobbler's wife did not remain idle, but plied her fists as hard as she could, and would undoubtedly have killed her if Mr Bek [the minister] had not arrived upon the scene and stated that he would take cognizance of the affair, whereupon they left off her.' We do not know what caused this outbreak of violence, but the neighbourhood is a lot more peaceful nowadays.

Next to Loubser House is Saxenhof, the sort of house more typical of the better-class survivors of Victorian suburbia than of Dorp Street, Stellenbosch. But this stately double-storey, with its ornate first-floor balcony, its fretted woodwork and cast iron, once was a typical Cape Dutch dwelling. The old H-pattern house that forms the basic fabric of the present building may have been built by the free burgher Pieter Saxe to whom the site was granted in 1704. Diagonally opposite at the corner of Ryneveld Street, on to which it fronts, is a house that undoubtedly contains the fabric of one of the oldest of all Stellenbosch houses – the Colonieshuis, or 'Colony House'. This was erected to the order of the court of landdrost and heemraden as public offices, or as a building that could be placed at the disposal of visiting officials or even hired out. In 1698, for instance, it was let to Jean du Plessis and his wife, Marie Buisset, the Huguenot progenitors of the family Du Plessis. Two years later the Colonieshuis was let to the Reverend Hercules van Loon, first full-time minister of the colony of Stellenbosch, who moved in with his wife, Maria Engelbrecht. This, then, became the first parsonage in Stellenbosch.

In view of the sad ending of the Reverend Hercules van Loon, it is worth taking a look at his wife, Maria. Adam Tas, writing

in 1706, mentions 'the widow van Loon, that haughty, sour-faced woman'. The Reverend Engelbertus le Boucq, a troublesome and spiteful clergyman who was supposed to minister at Drakenstein, also had his opinion of her. For his money, Widow van Loon was a 'malicious and false blabber-mouth'. It seems that after her husband's death she and their small son, Philippus, were allowed to stay on in the Colonieshuis and that she sided with the Governor's faction when the burghers took action against him. Having moved to Cape Town, she was appointed overseer of the Company's gravediggers in 1710 and later that year married the secunde, Willem Helot, who became acting-governor and, eventually, was banished in disgrace. And what was the sad ending of the Reverend van Loon? Returning to Stellenbosch from his farm, Hercules Pilaar near Joostenberg, one day in 1704, he dismounted and, somewhere alone on the lonely veld, he 'cut his own throat with a penknife'. Peter Kolb adds that this occurred 'without anyone ever having known for what reason he had fallen into that despair'. Perhaps Maria had nothing to do with it but, whatever the reason, the Reverend Hercules van Loon saw the Colonieshuis no more.

Van Loon's successor, Henricus Beck, declined to occupy this Colonieshuis and chose another, of which no trace remains, at the corner of Church and Ryneveld streets. For more than a century, Van Loon's former parsonage served as the official residence of the secretary to the college of landdrost and

Left *D'Ouwe Werf, a country inn at the heart of old Stellenbosch, is built over the site of the first church.*

Right *The warm interior of D'Ouwe Werf is furnished with a variety of beautiful antique furniture.*

heemraden, one of the incumbents being Peter Kolb. If we pass by the side of this house along Dorp Street, we come to Number 182 – the Old Reading Room. With its simple gable and attractive fanlight above double doors, this started out as public offices erected around 1815. It was also hired out for cultural events and, since its name is explicitly given as 'Reading Room', we may assume that it was the meeting place of a Dutch reading circle and also of the later book club established by Humphrey McLachlan as an adjunct to his school. Indeed, the building served as a school, but its greatest distinction is that in it the decision was taken to found a gymnasium from which the Victoria College and, ultimately, the University of Stellenbosch were to develop.

A part of the University is the Theological Seminary; it stands across Dorp Street from the Old Reading Room and squarely at the head of Drostdy Street. This is the site of the old drostdy and of Simon van der Stel's island encampment. The first drostdy was destroyed in the fire of 1710 but in the Village

Museum pictures and a collage made in about 1830 show what the second drostdy looked like. This splendid building, with its grandly exuberant gable, lies buried within the present Theological Seminary which itself has been rebuilt several times.

BEYOND DORP STREET

Away from the shade and splendour of Dorp Street, the next most obvious focus of old Stellenbosch is the Braak. This village square has been variously named King's Square, Queen's Square and even Adderley Square. In the end, though, it always came back to being Die Braak – the fallow ground. Like Cape Town's Grand Parade, the Braak has been parade ground, fair ground, sports field and general meeting-place. It was also, earlier this century, very nearly the site of the new town hall, but reason and public indignation prevailed.

The village fair had its origins in Simon van der Stel's visit to the embryonic village in 1686. It happened to be his birthday, 14 October, and it was arranged that he would spend the next

one at Stellenbosch, where in due course he was honoured by a parade of burghers, both mounted and on foot, and the firing of a salute from their long, flintlock muskets. His next and last birthday visit was in 1698, but the idea of an October festival continued for many years, and has recently been revived.

Petrus Borcherds tells us of the festival, or *kermis*, that attended the military parade of 1794, the year before the first British occupation of the Cape. (The British commander, General Sir James Craig, described the Braak as 'a place of recreation and an ornament to the village'.) Burgher cavalry 'used to exercise annually in the village, on the Braak, now Queen's-square,' wrote Borcherds. 'In the month of October, eight days were kept, devoted to drilling during the day, and cheerful meeting of parties in the evening. Every house was thrown open, and the inhabitants received exclusive privilege to sell cakes and refreshments during this period, which was known under the name of "de Kermis".

'Several families from Cape Town and the environs spent the kermis at Stellenbosch… The select visitors, the landdrost and notables of the village were assembled on the day, 24th October (optrek dag), in an alcove of trees, called the Tent, of which the remnant is still to be seen, facing the square by the side of a brook leading to the village watermill. [This was at the southern end of the Braak, just behind the Rhenish Church, in the area still known as Molen Plein.] The commissary sat in state in an arm chair, whilst the corps defiled by, the officers passing the tent saluting.' Some of the Braak's buildings that looked down on that scene look down on it today.

Most distinctive is the kruithuis, or arsenal, that was built, then on the edge of town, in 1777. The burghers of Stellenbosch had asked for it in 1686, almost a century earlier but bureaucracy rarely moves fast. The first question involved its position. Generally, when a frontier settlement needed gunpowder, it needed it in a hurry, so one faction favoured having the arsenal as close to home as possible. The pessimist school argued that if it was so situated and accidentally blew up, it would take the entire village with it. Finally built, it was of massive solidity with a vaulted roof of brick and stone the better to contain any accidental explosion. Additional security was provided by the high blast-wall built around the arsenal. The bell tower is a later addition. When the little building had outlived its usefulness as an arsenal, it became a market, and then home to the local fire brigade, before being restored and re-opened as a museum of Stellenbosch militaria.

Like the arsenal, the nearby church of St Mary-on-the-Braak started without its bell tower, which was added in 1884, some 30 years after the church was consecrated. Very much larger, and in a completely different style, is the Rhenish Church, inaugurated in 1824, when the ceremony was attended by notables including the Governor, Lord Charles Somerset, whose days in power were already numbered. On the western perimeter of the Braak, the Rhenish Institute, now an art centre, started out as a west-facing, single-storeyed, H-shaped and gabled dwelling, probably before 1787.

Burgher House, so named for no very clear reason, was built by Anthonie Fick in 1797, but what name he gave it is no longer

Far left *Smooth thatch contrasts with a fussy, moulded little pediment in Herte Street.*

Centre left *Perhaps only sun-baked, these exposed bricks have begun to dissolve in the rain.*

Left *With shuttered windows like eyelids closed in repose, a Herte Street cottage dreams in the sunlight.*

Right *Herte Street, with its long row of 'slave cottages' was to have been the centre of a silk-producing industry in the 1860s.*

known. It was built to the H-plan, and was later greatly extended, although the extensions have not survived. For some 40 years Burgher House was the home of the Reverend Paulus Lückhoff, the Rhenish missionary, and after his retirement in 1878, continued to serve as mission parsonage. Serene in its immaculate garden with a gently lisping fountain, Burgher House has been described as perhaps the most delicately proportioned building in South Africa. Nor is that its only claim to attention: it is also the headquarters of the conservation group, Historical Homes of South Africa, and has a section open to the public as a museum.

The Coachman's Cottage in Alexander Street never was a coachman's cottage but the name sticks, despite that. It has a front dormer gable, rather like that of Mon Repos at Oude Libertas, but the house is much older, having been built around 1791. The splendidly ornate end-gables make one wonder whether there was not, originally, a similar gable in front. The builder and original owner was Jan Lankhoff, a tailor who, sad

to say, had gone insolvent by 1801. Today the Coachman's Cottage is the property of the Anglican Church. Next door, Laetitia, a double-storeyed building with a Georgian façade, was once very like the Coachman's Cottage but was given its upper floor – and a flat, fireproof roof – after the fire of 1803.

Strolling away from the Braak down Market Street, you soon come to Herte Street on your left. Nobody is really sure about the derivation of this street name. The most popular guess is that it is a corrupted form of Hertzog, given in honour of W F Hertzog, who began work as a surveyor in Stellenbosch in 1813. The view over the garden wall of the Rhenish complex opposite the cottages and towards the distant mountains is one of the grandest that Stellenbosch has to offer. The complex consists of the parsonage and outbuildings, most of them already in existence by 1817 when surveyor Hertzog produced a street plan of Stellenbosch showing all buildings. What you see here today is the result of one of the most ambitious and successful restoration projects undertaken in the town. Over the years the buildings fell upon lean times. Thatch was replaced with corrugated iron, which meant that the stately gables were clipped into simple, plain triangles. Little Victorian frills and a veranda of hideous grandeur were tacked on to the front of the parsonage. Fortunately, old photographs as well as skilful on-site detective work resulted in restoration that was truly authentic.

Very much simpler but no less charming are the cottages on the opposite side of Herte Street. There is a story that many of these were built in the 1830s to house recently liberated slaves, although this has not been proven. Many of the Herte Street cottages, certainly, were occupied by 'people of colour' for generations until they were obliged to give up their homes by the implementation of the (now repealed) Group Areas Act. Their tenancy is believed to date from the 1860s when a Rhenish missionary, the Reverend Johannes Hahn, bought the row of cottages and installed in them members of his congregation. The Reverend Johannes Hahn also started a silk-spinning industry, but like similar ventures in Cape Town (where Spin Street is a reminder) and at Knysna, this was a failure. The house in Herte Street which was occupied by this good man no longer exists but Number 17, dating from before 1817, was its annexe.

Back in Market Street, turn away from the Braak, and you are looking at gracious Van der Bijl House behind its massive, spreading oaks. Built in about 1804, it incorporates fabric of De Oude Basthuis, or tannery, that was partially destroyed in the fire of 1803 and was afterwards raised to double-storey height and given a flat roof. The little storeroom and pigeon loft are thought to have been part of the old tannery. Pigeon lofts or dovecotes are not infrequently found on farms in the district, but are, of course, rare in the town. Also rare here are gentle bends in the roads which tend to be more or less straight and to cross at right angles. Now, Van der Bijl House stands on a gentle bend on Market Street which it is believed was constructed to follow the wagon-road into the town from the Overberg. The wagons would have rolled down Old Strand Road, turned for a short while into Dorp Street and then into Market Street as they headed for the Braak. Why the bend? Perhaps there was some obstruction, such as a bush, but one has only to look at a veld footpath or cattle-track from the air to see how it curves and turns for reasons that today are no longer apparent. Johannes van der Bijl, who moved to this house from his father's farm Schoongezicht (now renamed Lanzerac) in 1848, was a pioneer in the field of tree-grafting to obtain better fruits.

Adjacent to Van der Bijl House is De Eiken at Number 39, once the home of architect and painter, Carl Otto Hager, designer of the old Lutheran Church in Dorp Street. He did not design this house, however: it appears on the town plan of 1817 and he arrived in Stellenbosch only in 1841. Here he married and here he worked, as artist, architect, shopkeeper and photographer, and here he died, after living in Stellenbosch for about 57 years. It is worth recalling his account of his arrival in Stellenbosch, although it was written some years afterwards. Depressed at having failed to make a living in Cape Town, he had decided to see something of the interior of the country before returning to Germany. 'I got down from the wagon and beheld the distant view of the beautiful mountains of Stellenbosch, Jonkershoek and Drakenstein; before me lay a spacious valley planted with vineyards and plantations, and in its centre was the village of Stellenbosch. At that distance it looked like Paradise. I felt a surge of nostalgia; I thought of my fatherland, and some prophetic sense told me that this would become the place where I would find peace on earth.' It was by no means peace without a struggle but, for Hager at any rate, the assessment of Stellenbosch as Paradise proved to be justified.

Hager claimed that, before moving to Stellenbosch, he had designed St Mary's Roman Catholic Church (now cathedral) on Looiers Plein, adjoining Stal Plein, in Cape Town. The official history of that church records that the architect was 'a Mr Sparman, a German', and only Sparman's name is mentioned

Left *The fruits of toil and the soil are offered on this vegetable stall in the town.*

Right *A cheerful seller anticipates a ready market for his fine blooms.*

in the diary of Bishop Grimley, who was consecrated shortly before his arrival in Cape Town in 1861. Sparman apparently failed to give full satisfaction, however, and it is possible that the church design was a joint venture of two fellow countrymen. And there can be no mistaking the severely Gothic lines – Hager's favourite style – of the cathedral, to which the tower was added only in the 1920s. In addition to the old Lutheran Church, Hager's work in Stellenbosch includes the Moederkerk of the Dutch Reformed congregation. He may also have designed the Ou Hoofgebou, formerly Victoria College.

Shortly after his arrival in Stellenbosch, Hager stayed at the lodging house run by Wouter Wium in Church Street. This was a single-storeyed building with gable and thatched roof which, heavily disguised, still stands as D'Ouwe Werf and, as a restaurant and country house hotel, continues a long tradition of hospitality believed to have started in 1802. The history of the site, however, goes back still further to 1687 when a little rectangular church, complete with belfry, was built here. It was destined for destruction, together with the melancholy graves that surrounded it, in the fire of 1710. When the new church was built, a different site – that of the present Moederkerk – was chosen, and the ruined church was abandoned. Only some 70 years later was the former churchyard divided into building-plots and, when excavations revealed traces of human remains, the inevitable ghost stories did the rounds. None, however, seems particularly scary or well documented but the remains of Stellenbosch's first church are still to be seen beneath the rear part of D'Ouwe Werf.

One of the buildings to rise on the site of the old church was Wium's boarding house. When it was built is not certain, but a drawing made in 1889 shows that the gable bore the date 1802. Among the distinguished guests of 1860 was the Governor, Sir George Grey, who was accompanying young Prince Alfred, son of Queen Victoria, on a short inland tour. 'Affie', as the prince was known, spent the night at the parsonage of Reverend Johannes Neethling. Sometime early in the 1890s the house was converted to its present double-storey configuration, and renamed Arcadia, by which it was known – especially to the 'parlour boarders' – for many years.

Another old-time boarding house is sited just across the road, at 33 Church Street. This was known as The Oaks, Quarrywoods and doubtless other names before it acquired its present designation of Coopmanhuijs, after Bartholomeus Co-opman, a blacksmith and 'gun-maker' who, in 1713, was the first person to hold title to the property. By the 1880s the owner of this house, by then much altered and given a second

storey, was Hubertus Elffers. Although he was a teacher at the Gymnasium, Elffers saw no wrong in enticing boarders to his own home with a quaintly worded advertisement that offered accommodation to 'youths desirous of studying seriously and devotedly, who therefore do not belong in boarding houses where they are left to themselves, lacking all supervision'. No doubt the implication of 'supervision' impressed parents of school-going boys.

Eastwards from Coopmanhuijs – that is, in the direction of the Moederkerk that dominates the end of Church Street – and on the right-hand side of the road is the Hofmeyr Hall. Also known as the CJV Hall, it was originally referred to as the YMCA Hall and was designed as a Christian meeting-place for the young by the architect R M Robertson. But the inspiration behind it was the Reverend Nicolaas Hofmeyr who, appointed one of the first professors of the Theological Seminary in 1859, retained that post until 1907. Born in Welgemeend, one of the old Table Valley farmsteads that still stands, he studied theology in Holland and became a lively preacher of the 'revivalist' school, as well as a campaigner for total abstinence from alcohol. In the heart of the winelands, the propagation of abstinence was not well received, but in the end, affection for this good and sincerely religious man overcame hostility. Hofmeyr felt especially drawn to young people – he and his wife, Maria Louw, had no fewer than five sons and six daughters – and he was an ideal choice for the new Theological Seminary in Stellenbosch. In addition to his ordinary duties, he held Bible classes in his own home next to the site of the present hall, even putting himself to the bother and expense of re-modelling his home to accommodate still more students. Eventually, around 1900, the hall was built, in an oddly proportioned sort of Greek Revival style complete with vague, toga-clad figures painted in the tympanum, or the space enclosed by the triangular pediment.

On the same side of the road and just across Ryneveld Street, but far removed in mood from the Hofmeyr Hall, is frivolously named Maidens' Hope. This was the sobriquet given to their boarding house, at 47 Church Street, by early students of Victoria College. Lest they be thought vain, they also called it Oude Mannen-tehuis, or 'old men's home', and it is presently known as Van Niekerk House, after an early owner. This is a double-storeyed dwelling that was probably built as such, and not raised to extra heights from gabled, single-storey level, as were so many other Stellenbosch houses.

Ryneveld Street is one of Stellenbosch town's earliest streets, although it was once known as De Groote Kerkstraat because it formed one of the boundaries of the original churchyard. The intersection with the present Church Street is thought to be the town's oldest street corner. On one side stands modest Schreuderhuis, now a part of the Village Museum, and on the other is the rather grand – and perhaps strangely named, for Stellenbosch – Devonshire House. Like the more homely sounding Van Niekerk House round the corner, Devonshire House was built as a double-storey from the start, in about 1850. It was once the home of the chairman of the board of the Stellenbosch Bank (not to be confused with the Stellenbosch District Bank, which was founded in 1882 and is still in existence). The Stellenbosch Bank was one of some 30 Cape local banks founded between 1836 and 1873, every one of which was liquidated by 1890. The turn of the Stellenbosch Bank came in 1877, shareholders having met the previous year 'to consider the deplorable state of the Bank's affairs'. That they were truly deplorable is shown by the fact that the bank's deficiency was no less than £48 940 and that a shareholder's meeting should have been called when the deficiency had reached the relatively modest sum of £2 917. Sad to relate, the chairman himself – J Wege, who had been on the first committee of the Stellenbosch Gymnasium – owed the bank £16 473 and, even sadder, committed suicide in his lovely home. But Devonshire House has borne this sorrow well,

and looks calmly with almost identical facades on both Church and Ryneveld streets, although the postal authorities have decreed that its address is Ryneveld Street.

Across Church Street and over the road is Morkel House, probably the oldest of all Stellenbosch buildings, although it was originally a wine cellar, not a dwelling. After the destruction of the church in the fire of 1710, its owner, Jan Botma, offered its use as a temporary place of worship. That wine cellar, which did duty as church until 1724, was the basic fabric of Morkel House, later acquired by the church council and then the colony of Stellenbosch, to serve as an official residence. In Victorian times it suffered the fate of so many Cape Dutch houses and lost its thatch and gables. It was then that it gained its two front doors that, during restoration in the 1960s, were allowed to remain as an attractive feature of the façade.

Go north along Ryneveld Street – that is, away from Dorp Street – and you come to busy Plein Street that leads from the Braak and, to the right, becomes Van Riebeeck Street. Along the north side runs the millstream, *Het Molen Water*, its days of glory immortalized nearby in panels of sculpted bronze. Although its flow no longer turns a millwheel, it stirs remembrance of a slower, gentler time, and an appreciation that so much of Stellenbosch, lovingly shaped by many hands over many years, remains still to be enjoyed.

The Café Cat, sculpted by Nerine Desmond,
commemorates an official decision that cats should not
be allowed in restaurants.

*'I was sent to a Dutch school under
the master Georg Knoop, the parish clerk...'*

TO LEARN AND TO SERVE

_____ IF THE EARLY SETTLEMENT along the banks of the Eerste River seemed a long way from the nearest centre of European civilization at the Castle on the shores of Table Bay, how much further removed it must have seemed from Holland. So, understandably, it was not long before these remote settlers – pioneers of pioneers – stirred themselves to try to bring something of their age-old heritage to their new isolation. A letter – undated but certainly written in 1683 – to Commander Simon van der Stel contains their plea. Styling themselves residents of 'the colony or settlement on the Eerste River in Africa', they requested that they be sent a schoolmaster cum sick-comforter. The sick-comforter was an official employed by the Dutch East India Company whose duty it was to visit members of the church congregation in times of illness or bereavement and also to conduct a school where basic education would be given.

At the Cape, a school for slaves was established in 1658. This was no act of charity but was intended to increase the value of the slaves to their owners and to the Company. To encourage his slave pupils to attend classes, the sick-comforter, Pieter van der Stael, was instructed by the Council of Policy to offer each one, every school day, a tot of brandy and five centimetres of tobacco.

The first school for the education of the children of Dutch settlers was started only in 1663, with sick-comforter Ernestus Back as teacher. Families that could afford to do so would later hire private tutors for their children – Frans van der Stel, for instance, employed one Hendrik Noord as 'leermeester in de Musicque'. The best that the burghers of the colony along the Eerste River could do, meanwhile, was to apply for the services of a sick-comforter. They justified their request by declaring that their remote situation had deprived them of spiritual comfort and had lost their children the opportunity to acquire a knowledge of reading, writing and other matters. Knowing full well that the Company was prompted principally by commercial motives, they tactfully added that the acquisition of such knowledge would render the children of greater value to their church and to the Company. Simon van der Stel, to whom their plea was addressed, was undoubtedly made to feel that if their request were not granted, his inland colony would not survive. His

Left *The annual rugby intervarsity against the University
of Cape Town draws enthusiastic student spectators.*

Above *Study décor is a matter of personal choice,
as long as it oils the cogs of thought.*

Above *It just might be because they're students, or it might have something to do with a physics demonstration.*

Right *Traditionally, this is how students – here seen passing Church House – get around Stellenbosch. It may be quaint and old fashioned, but it helps to avoid the parking problems that plague other universities.*

response, approved by the Council of Policy, was to send them sick-comforter Sijbrand Mancadan.

Mancadan had once been a minister of the Dutch Reformed Church in Holland. However, he was suspended from the ministry in 1677, re-instated, and then permanently dismissed in 1682. Despite this unfortunate record, he was nevertheless employed by the Dutch East India Company and, the next year, found himself at the Cape. His little schoolhouse, which was also his home, was the first building in the future town of Stellenbosch, as distinct from the farming settlement, and was probably situated on the site of the present town hall on the corner of Andringa and Plein streets. Perhaps seeing the school as the start of a more closely knit and permanent settlement, Simon van der Stel took a lively interest in its progress. In place of the brandy and tobacco doled out to conscientious slave pupils, Mancadan's young charges, on the instruction of the Commander himself, were encouraged to be diligent by the award of modest prizes each year. At the prize-giving ceremony, each child was also presented with a piece of cake, the size of the slice being in proportion to the amount of effort exerted in learning by the particular pupil. Mancadan showed his gratitude by assembling his young scholars under a banner of welcome on the Commander's birthday when Van der Stel happened to be visiting the colony.

Although his little displays may have gained him brief favour with the Commander, Mancadan soon fell foul of the burghers. At the end of 1687 the college of landdrost and heemraden wrote to Van der Stel complaining bitterly about Mancadan's drunkenness and inattention to his duties. In addition to being teacher and sick-comforter, he was secretary to his accusers and, apparently, gave poor service in all spheres. He had married earlier that year and, in response to the complaint against him, submitted his own sad little petition in which he admitted to taking a glass too many on occasions. He begged the Commander and Council of Policy to consider his wife and defenceless children (some, presumably, from an earlier marriage) and to bear in mind that he was an old man. Despised by the burghers of Stellenbosch, who withheld their children from his school and shut the door on him when he called at their homes, Mancadan nevertheless stayed in office, at least as secretary, but his name disappears from the record after 1694 when Jan Jansz Swart was appointed as the new sick-comforter. Either the burghers of Stellenbosch demanded an unusually high moral standard of their teacher and sick-comforter or they had bad luck in those chosen for the post. Whatever the reason, in 1700 they were complaining about

Swart, too, and requesting that a 'more decorous man' be sent to them. This turned out to be Jan Mahieu who, in the tradition of his predecessors, also came in for his share of criticism.

Diarist Adam Tas, for instance, found Mahieu to be 'voluble' and 'tedious in all matters, even in his manner of speech'. The house that he was building (on the site of Mankadan Flats in Dorp Street) was also criticized as tedious. As secretary to the college of landdrost and heemraden, Mahieu appears to have kept meticulous records – especially when compared with the messy scribblings of Mancadan and Swart – but despite this Landdrost Mulder openly called him a fraud. The problem was not solved by Mahieu's removal from the post of schoolmaster and he continued as secretary to the college of landdrost and heemraden until he was replaced in 1711 by Peter Kolb. For several years Stellenbosch had no teacher but in 1708 Bastiaan Cheval was appointed to fill the vacancy and also that of sexton to the church. Here at last was someone about whom Tas was unlikely to carp too seriously for Cheval was married to Cornelia Hüsing, daughter of Tas's uncle and sometime employer. By the time of Cheval's appointment, however, there was no longer a suitable schoolhouse available so lessons were given in the church, which was itself fated to be destroyed by fire within a few years.

The public schools at the Cape and at Stellenbosch were open to all pupils, the children of Dutch settlers as well as those of slaves and free blacks, and teachers continued to be officials of the church and the Company. On rare occasions, Company servants were allowed to be employed by free burghers and sometimes acted as private tutors. Nevertheless, the standard of education was not satisfactory, nor was there any definite legislation to regulate matters concerning it. The situation was not helped by the fact that the governor, Louis van Assenburg, had died in 1711 and for the next few years the colony was under the acting-governorship of Willem Helot, the secunde or deputy-governor. The little that is known of Helot does not suggest that he might have given his undivided attention to the matter of educating the children of the colony. Within a few months of the arrival of the new governor, Helot was to be accused of dishonesty and neglect of duty, stripped of his rank and salary, dismissed from the Company's service and, with his assets confiscated, dispatched in disgrace to Holland.

The governor who had so abruptly and completely brought about the fall of Willem Helot was Mauritz Pasques de Chavonnes who, before joining the Company's service, had been a career officer in the Dutch army. It was through his initiative that the first school regulations were promulgated in August 1714. If anything, De Chavonnes was perhaps a little ahead of his time, or rather ahead of the colony's time, in establishing at the Cape a school in which Dutch and Latin were taught. Lack of support from the unsophisticated burghers and Company's servants forced this institution to close although it lasted for 16 years – but others survived even longer.

In terms of De Chavonnes' ordinance, no person could teach unless he had been examined by the governor and Council of Policy and found by them to be worthy in both morals and learning. Control of school affairs in the entire colony was vested in a body known as the Heeren Scholarchen which consisted of the deputy-governor, the captain of the garrison and the minister of the Dutch Reformed Church in Cape Town. In the outlying districts, though, teachers continued to be approved by the local consistories, or church councils, which all had their own tastes and peculiarities. A later applicant for the post of schoolmaster at Stellenbosch was turned down, not because of any moral shortcomings or gaps in his education, but because his singing was not up to the standard required by the consistory. The duties of a schoolmaster were still not entirely divorced from obligations to the church, one of which was to act as voorleser and lead the singing of the psalms. The church was particularly pleased with the musical abilities of Cheval's successors, Jacobus de Rens in 1716 and Antoine Alexandre Faure, who arrived at the Cape in 1714 and was appointed teacher five years later.

Far left *The oak-dappled sunlight suggests a pub in rural England, but the gable proclaims that this is Stellenbosch.*

Left *Taking your coffee alfresco means you're still part of the passing scene.*

Right *The barrel-like objects with the bright red hoops are old wine-presses, appropriate décor for one of the town's leading rendezvous for students, business people and visitors alike.*

Left *Drip mouldings above veranda height tell us the stoeps of the Centre for Legal Aid were added as an afterthought.*

Above *There's time for some refreshment – and friendship – between lectures.*

Faure, a French Huguenot who had grown up in Holland, arrived at the Cape as a soldier of the Dutch East India Company. His good record, his proficiency in Dutch and, of course, his excellent voice secured him the post of teacher that he was to fill to the satisfaction of all for more than 15 years. He was followed by his son, Abraham, who upheld the Faure tradition as teacher until 1761 when he gave up schoolmastering to become secretary to the college of landdrost and heemraden. This had formerly been more or less bound to the teaching post, to the detriment of both functions.

In one respect, however, there was an ominous sign of a return to the bad old days. Faure's successor, Christiaan Krijnauw, was appointed sick-comforter and voorleser as well as schoolmaster and, while the church had no complaints regarding his conduct, the little school suffered from its teacher's growing neglect. Only after parents began to refuse to allow their children to attend lessons did the church council act and as a result Krijnauw was sternly rebuked. Perhaps he had also been neglecting the singing, because in 1773 the verger, a man named Reinierke, was granted permission by the church council to start a school for the express purpose of improving the singing of the psalms. Krijnauw's rebuke came in 1779, after which he presumably mended his ways to some extent because he remained as schoolmaster until 1783. His successor, for a brief period, was Gilles de Korte who was followed, in 1785, by one who gave satisfaction not only to church council and parents, but even to his pupils.

One of these pupils was Petrus Borchardus Borcherds, son of the minister, and the much-admired schoolmaster was Georg Knoop. After retiring as resident magistrate and civil commissioner of Cape Town in 1857, Petrus Borcherds wrote his memoirs of 'occurrences from early life to advanced age...' which were published in 1861. (A facsimile edition appeared just over a century later.) Knoop had successfully run a school in Cape Town before accepting, at Stellenbosch, the post of teacher, combined with that of voorleser and leader of singing in the church. Young Borcherds was to remember him and his school with great clarity. 'At the age of seven years,' he wrote, 'I was sent to a Dutch school under the master Georg Knoop, the parish clerk, commonly called the Dominie, and remained under his tuition until my tenth year... The master was a gray-haired man, of florid complexion, and lively eye, precise to a nicety, remarkably clean in appearance and habit, wearing spectacles, and generally a fine linen cap and chintz gown. He sat at his elevated little table, with a library at the back, and the various scholastic implements, such as rulers, pens &c.,

Left *The symmetry and serene dignity of the façade of the university's C L Marais Library are a marked contrast to the carefree craziness of rag or 'jool'. The hidden seriousness, though, is that money is collected for deserving charities.*

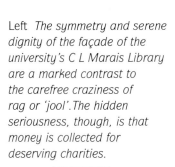

spread before him, while the instruments of discipline then in use hung on the wall by his side.

'Silence was the watchword, and eyes constantly fixed on the books was the rule. The school was opened and closed with prayer. The Bible was first read, then spelling, reading, arithmetic, and writing classes were put in action, the seniors taking the lessons of the juniors, the master taking the higher class. Wednesday and Saturday were especially destined for religious instruction in the catechism and the Hellenbroek. Attendance was regular, from eight to eleven in the morning, and from one to four in the afternoon. On Wednesday and Saturday half-holidays were allowed, three days during Easter and Whitsun weeks, and eight during Christmas, – and these were the only holidays during the year; the last included New Year's Day.

'Thus were the youth of the day plainly instructed in our village, in a manner both suited to their future various secular occupations in life, generally occupations in husbandry, or some mechanical craft, and to qualify them for admission as members of the Dutch Reformed Church, then the predominant and only one in the village; and this last was considered the highest degree of qualification.'

Georg Knoop died in 1800 while the Cape was under British military occupation. Educational matters were left to the Scholarchs assisted now by the Burgher Senate which had been formed in 1796 to replace the old Council of Policy. During the brief administration of the Batavian Republic, from 1803 to 1806, Commissioner-General J A de Mist published an ordinance that, for the first time, made education the responsibility of the state, rather than the church, a concept that drew opposition from many burghers, especially those in outlying areas. But this interregnum was too brief for many of De Mist's progressive schemes to be implemented and in Stellenbosch the church continued in control of the village school.

At the not-too-distant village of 'the Paarl', meanwhile, Jan van Lindenbaum had cast a fairly wide net by starting a private boarding school with a relatively sophisticated curriculum. In 1806 Van Lindenbaum applied to the Council of Scholarchs for permission to increase the number of his pupils from 30 to 50. In reply, the Council requested him to move to the larger village of Stellenbosch where it considered his institution would be of greater public benefit. To this Van Lindenbaum readily agreed. A prospectus announced that the new school was for 'young gentlemen from eight to sixteen years of age', and that subjects to be taught would include Dutch, French, arithmetic, geography and mathematics. Drawing, English and music were optional, and would cost extra. Religious instruction would be

Above *Like faithful steeds at a hitching post, students' bicycles await the end of a lecture period.*

Right *This is part of the main campus of the university, where modern developments include such facilities as an underground library. Twelve faculties offer a total of some 150 degree courses, in addition to those for diplomas.*

Left *Matie athletes at Stellenbosch have established an enviable record on field and track. Their stadium at Coetzenburg has facilities for more than 20 types of sport.*

Right *Limbering up in this sylvan setting is one of the pleasant aspects of staying fit.*

given under the auspices of the local minister, and reports on their children's progress would be submitted to parents every quarter. The school day began at six o'clock when, after cleaning their shoes, the boys were to wash, dress and attend prayers. Breakfast was at seven o'clock, and lessons began an hour later and continued until 11h30 when there was a break. After lunch, lessons resumed at two o'clock and continued until six. Supper was at eight o'clock and lights out, after closing prayers, was at nine. In all, a fairly full and useful day.

Unfortunately this promising venture lasted for only a little more than a year. Because of financial problems, the school was converted to a day establishment and opened to girls as well as boys, with a deputy teacher, J de Huyserbeck, having charge of the girls' section. Further misfortune followed, with De Huyserbeck and Van Lindenbaum becoming embroiled in a quarrel that came close to ending in a street fight (on a Sunday, of all days). The result was that the school was divided, but by the end of 1811 both institutions had closed. In the same year Sir John Cradock became governor of the Cape and set about giving his serious attention to education. He had, indeed, cause

to be concerned. Although the figures for Stellenbosch are not known precisely, in the district of Graaff-Reinet out of some 3 400 children of school-going age only about 100 actually attended school or were receiving instruction privately. Once again the church was closely allied to education and schools were placed directly under local authorities which usually consisted of the magistrate and the church council. Teaching was to be undertaken by the verger or voorleser, once these had been examined in Cape Town and found equal to the task. These schools became known as 'kosterskole', after the Dutch word for verger – koster. The Colonial Government was responsible for their salaries, in addition to which they received half of the school fees paid and a grant of land. Schoolmasters competent to teach the English language received an additional cash award.

In 1813 the Bible and School Commission was set up under the patronage of the governor but despite its findings, promulgations and recommendations, schooling in Stellenbosch – and elsewhere – did no more than stagger along. For this, the Bible and School Commission was partly to blame as most of its members were ministers who, somewhat short-sightedly, were more concerned with distributing bibles than with teaching those who received them to read. Some blame for lack of progress lay also with parents, most of whom believed that when a child could manage to read and write a little its useful education was complete. In Stellenbosch, however, a group of parents showed a more responsible spirit and submitted a petition of protest.

The Cradock system was not working well and, although he may have been obliged to teach under difficult conditions, the Stellenbosch schoolmaster, Gerrit van Coppenhagen, was failing badly in his task. Eventually, in addition to voicing mere protest, Stellenbosch parents demanded to be allowed to open a private school with a more comprehensive curriculum than that offered at the public school. Permission to do so was duly granted to Nicolaas Janssen, a German resident in Stellenbosch since 1806, and from about 1820 he ran a private school, assisted by his daughter, Cornelia, in his own home in Church Street. The house had two front doors, one leading to the schoolroom and the other to the family's living quarters and the studio where Cornelia taught music. Janssen's school flourished while the public school continued to limp along, losing pupils also to the free English school started in 1822 by the Colonial Government as part of the policy of Anglicization. This was a scheme that was applied not only to schools and the public service, but also to the Dutch Reformed Church. Ministers to serve in it were no longer sought in Holland but were recruited in Scotland in the hope that they would convert their future congregations to the English language. In the event, the ministers themselves were converted to Dutch and later to Afrikaans and this part of the plan, at any rate, turned out to be a dismal failure.

THE SCOTTISH INFLUENCE

Had the great drive to convert the colony to all things English been implemented under a governor less haughty and autocratic than Lord Charles Somerset, it might have had a better chance of succeeding. He was born into a wealthy family descended, albeit by an illegitimate line, from England's King Edward III who, interestingly enough, introduced English as the language of the law courts in place of French in 1362. At the Cape, Lord Charles made English the language of the local courts, too, but had less luck with the schools. He had six teachers brought from Scotland in 1822, among them James Rose Innes, one of the teaching profession's most dedicated servants of all time.

Another teacher was Archibald Brown, a graduate of the University of Aberdeen and destined for the government free school in Stellenbosch. His school stood on the post office site, at the corner of Bird and Plein streets and although it started well, he was simply too unbendingly – and one suspects, arrogantly – British to be accepted by the local people. According to Erasmus Smit, missionary teacher and Voortrekker-to-be, Brown was too free in his use of the cane. With the deliberate phasing out of Dutch in preparation for the entrenchment of English as the sole official language of the Cape, attendance at the English free schools gradually fell away, except in Uitenhage and Graaff-Reinet where Rose Innes and William Robertson, respectively, had sympathetically integrated with the local communities. In 1832 Brown returned to Cape Town to resign, which he managed to do in time to avoid being dismissed. What became of his successor, Robert Saunders, is not clear, but when reorganization took place following the formation of the Cape Education Department in 1839, his name was no longer on the rolls. James Rose Innes, Brown's erstwhile colleague, later became the first superintendent-general of education for the Cape Colony.

With the implementation of yet another new system, which this time encouraged participation and contribution from the local community, more new teachers arrived from Scotland.

Above *Maties play hard, and this one, down but not out, is watched over by a solicitous team member.*

Right *In splashes of sunlight and water, a well-muscled student sends his canoe surging forward.*

They had been recruited by the astronomer Sir John Herschel who had lately returned to Great Britain from the Cape. This time, before being let loose on up-country pupils, the new teachers had to spend two months in Cape Town to acquire a grounding in the Dutch language which they were to use in teaching 'as the Superintendent-General shall prescribe'. Scottish teachers were preferred, as were clergymen, 'on account of the readiness with which they have been known to assimilate to the customs and usage of [Dutch-speaking colonists] and the comparative ease with which they acquire a knowledge of their language'. Among the young Scotsmen who arrived was Humphrey McLachlan.

His school, in a part of the Old Reading Room, was opened with high hopes – there were no fewer than 74 pupils – and some ceremony by the civil commissioner, Daniel Johannes van Ryneveld, in September 1840. But the room was too cramped and inadequately ventilated, and the grounds were too small. Having looked about the town for more promising premises, McLachlan fixed on the old slave school and former smallpox hospital, then derelict. Within a few months the school was satisfactorily installed in the building on the corner of Plein and Ryneveld streets which is now part of the Village Museum. This was not quite McLachlan's last piece of good fortune: his school achieved an excellent reputation although its master endured frustration upon frustration, often because his perfectly reasonable requests – such as that for globes and atlases – were turned down due to lack of funds. He took to drink for a while and was stricken by a great personal tragedy when his son John, who had acted temporarily as assistant teacher, committed suicide.

It was a letter published in *Het Volksblad* in Cape Town that sealed the fate of both McLachlan and his school. The anonymous writer alleged that there had been scanty attendance on the part of the teacher as well as a serious breakdown of discipline. After an investigation, the school was closed at the end of 1865 and Humphrey McLachlan, who had taught in Stellenbosch for 25 years, was placed on pension. He survived the closure of his school by only some 10 months, dying at the relatively early age of 54 years.

But the McLachlan influence was not done yet. Mrs McLachlan, fondly known as 'Ou Miesies' and her daughter, 'Miss Philippa', started their own private school for young ladies in Plein Street. Some 10 years later, when Mrs McLachlan announced that she was to close this establishment, the resultant outcry and concern led directly to the founding of the school that became Bloemhof School for Girls.

STEPS TO HIGHER EDUCATION

In the 19th century the separation of boys from girls at schools was regarded as desirable, despite the shortage of qualified teachers which the formation of a 'Normal School' for teacher training in Cape Town in 1842 did little to redress. The Roman Catholic Bishop of Cape Town, Thomas Grimley (whose special interest in education led him to bring the Marist Brothers and Dominican Sisters to the Cape to establish notable schools), declared, 'I think these schools of boys and girls together are most pernicious.' It was the Victorian era, after all, and Bishop Grimley was not alone in his opinion.

Dr Langham Dale, who became secretary-general of education in 1859 following Rose Innes's resignation, held similar views. 'I must express my doubts...' he said, 'whether the mixture of the sexes in so many of the established schools... has not a tendency to depress the moral tone of our youth.' Thus, when Mrs McLachlan indicated that her girls' school was about to close, it is not surprising there was some alarm in many quarters of the town. But another private school for girls, albeit a somewhat exclusive one, had already been in existence in Stellenbosch for some 15 years. At the time it was known as the Rheinisches Institut.

The Rhenish Missionary Society was founded in Germany in 1828 and in October of the following year was represented in South Africa when the Reverend Paulus Daniel Lückhoff and three other missionaries arrived in Cape Town. Within less than a month, Lückhoff was invited by the Hulpzending Vereeniging of Stellenbosch to work among its coloured and slave populations. Stellenbosch in due course became the main centre of the Rhenish Missionary Society, together with Rietfontein in the Clanwilliam district, which they renamed Wupperthal. As more missionaries with their wives and families arrived to work in Stellenbosch, it was felt that some institution should be established to give the children an education on the same lines as that provided in their fatherland. There was a reluctance to send the children, especially the girls, to Germany for their education since this entailed not only great expense but meant a prolonged break-up of the family.

And so, in 1860, a private school for girls was opened under headmistress Miss Bertha Voigt who had come from Germany especially to take up the post. The school building, which belonged to Lückhoff, was on the edge of the Braak in Alexander Street between Laetitia and the Coachman's Cottage. Pupils of this new Rheinisches Institut were instructed in German and in English. In the same year, the Rhenish missionaries decided to add to their land-holdings in the area. One of them, the Reverend G Terlinden, had acquired a dwelling on the south side of the kruithuis when he married the Widow Suijkerman in 1850. Now, 10 years later, he bought the adjoining premises – a single-storeyed Cape Dutch style house with outhouse – from the Anglican clergyman, the Reverend Frederick Carlyon. Terlinden was not a property speculator. He bought Carlyon's house to prevent its site from being used for the erection of a hotel which he considered an undesirable neighbour to the school and mission. When Terlinden died in 1862 he bequeathed both properties to the Institute which, just at that time, as boarding- and day-school, had outgrown its original premises. The original dwelling became the home of the Rhenish Primary School while Carlyon's former house, with a second storey added, was converted into the boarding

Left *Communication, whether with your fellow students or your lecture notes, is an important part of university life. The library auditorium is a favourite gathering place, especially on warm winter days.*

Right *The Theological Seminary occupies the site of Van der Stel's encampment on the 'island' in the Eerste River. This old, central section of the building was once affectionately described as 'gorgeously exuberant, in the best Monte Carlo tradition'.*

hostel. Today it houses the P J Olivier Art Centre. In addition to serving the needs of the school, this consolidation of property ownership made possible the lovely concentration of buildings that constitutes the 'Rhenish complex' today.

In 1893 the Rhenish Institute introduced a 'housekeeping school' – the first in the country to teach domestic science. In time, this created the phenomenon of 'parlour boarders', young ladies who had been educated elsewhere but who attended the Rhenish as a finishing school where they learnt how to run their own households. Other subjects it offered included typing and shorthand, art and music. In 1909, after resisting suggestions to amalgamate with other schools – suggestions which roused the greatest interest throughout Stellenbosch – the Rhenish Institute became a school under the Cape Education Department, with German being dropped in favour of English as a medium of instruction in 1922.

Success with the girls' school encouraged the founding of a similar institution for boys. The Reverend Wilhelm Alheit was summoned from the Rhenish mission station at Schietfontein (later Carnarvon) in 1865 to found a school for the sons of missionaries on the site of the present post office. His house, which was adjacent, served as hostel. With the establishment of these two schools just after the middle of the 19th century, Stellenbosch at last saw the stirrings that would lead to its great academic future. A strong feeling began to develop that what was wanted was not merely a good school, but an institution that would provide an as yet undefined higher

Left *Cool brass stirs old memories and creates some new ones.*

Right *The statue of J H Marais, former student and great benefactor, looks benevolently on modern successors.*

education. A prospectus submitted to the superintendent-general of education in 1859 states that 'it is proposed to change the Government School at Stellenbosch into a Collegiate Institution'. This may, in part, have been a response to the British Government's attitude to the flow of its trained teachers to the colonies. On this subject, Governor Sir George Grey was advised that Britain could not 'be a party to the engagement for service in the Colonies of Schoolmasters or Schoolmistresses trained in England at the expense of funds voted by Parliament, unless either the Schoolmaster or Mistress, or the Colony will repay to the Government the cost incurred in educating them'. However, Sir George did not offer to pay nor did this warning completely arrest the departure of teachers from Britain, but the threat was apparent.

And 1859 was also the year that saw the opening of the Theological Seminary of the Dutch Reformed Church. The little village of oaks and water furrows, it seemed, was set to become a university town although the past history of stumbles and hiccups in the course of general education probably did not allow for unbridled optimism that this desirable dream would come true. As it turned out, the seminary did indeed seem set for success within a relatively short time.

At the beginning, it was not possible for young men to pass directly from school to seminary without some intermediate higher instruction. This, at first, was provided by professors John Murray and Nicolaas Hofmeyr, but their real appointment was to the seminary itself and not to the preparation of prospective students. With Stellenbosch-born Johannes Henoch Neethling, newly appointed minister of the local Dutch Reformed Church congregation, Murray and Hofmeyr got together to consider the 'Collegiate Institution' mentioned in the prospectus later sent to Dr Langham Dale.

If things seemed to be in abeyance for the next few years it was simply because the triumvirate of Murray, Hofmeyr and Neethling realized that to persuade the government to see the projected 'Collegiate Institution' in a favourable light, the idea would first have to be sold to the people of Stellenbosch. And sold it was, principally by Neethling who extracted numerous promises of sponsorship from members of his congregation. With financial and general support assured, a bolder document appeared in 1863; entitled 'ZA Gymnasium te Stellenbosch' it contained a signed resolution 'to establish a Gymnasium for the proper instruction of the youth of Stellenbosch'. Little more than a month later, in January 1864, more than 40 subscribers, each of whom had pledged an annual amount of money for five years, met in the Old Reading Room that had seen the

inauguration of Humphrey McLachlan's little school almost a quarter of a century earlier.

But greater things were planned now. The Gymnasium was 'to provide sound instruction in all subjects pertaining to a civilized education, as well as preparation for the examination of admission to the Theological Seminary and for the Government examination for the Second Class Certificate in letters and Sciences'. (This Second Class Certificate was roughly equivalent to a BA degree, although there would not be an examining university until 1873 when the University of the Cape of Good Hope was established by royal charter from Queen Victoria. In the meanwhile, a government-appointed Colonial Board of Examiners did duty.) The next day Dr Dale received the Reverend Johannes Neethling who told him that the new committee of the Gymnasium was able to provide the financial and other guarantees to qualify the proposed institution for a government grant. It was to be named 'Het Stellen-

bosch-Gymnasium' or, as English was the official language of the colony, it would also be known as Stellenbosch First Class Undenominational School for Boys.

From its commencement, in March 1866, the Gymnasium was immeasurably boosted by amalgamation with the school of the Reverend Alheit whose boys made up more than half the nominal roll of 88. Alheit, with true Christian generosity, offered his services as a part-time teacher – not for any personal reward, but in exchange for free education for the sons of a number of missionaries. His offer was gratefully accepted by the committee and the Reverend W E Braid, who had come from Scotland as the first principal. (When Braid returned to Scotland a few years later, he was replaced by another Scot, the Reverend Charles Anderson.)

The finding of suitable premises was a problem until Neethling suggested to a friend that he should erect a building and then let it to the management committee of the Gymnasium.

The resultant structure, with its elegant portico giving it a unique character, is still known as the Old Gymnasium and stands as 120-122 Dorp Street. While it was being built, the pupils of the new Gymnasium were crammed into the Old Reading Room, but within less than 10 years the combined areas of both old and new premises became too small. The Gymnasium building was extended but Dorp Street was declared too noisy. So, repeating history, the committee settled on the old slave school which had also done duty as smallpox hospital and as McLachlan's establishment. Here, in what is now part of the Bletterman House complex of the Village Museum, the Gymnasium made its home for a while in 1874.

In this same year Mrs McLachlan announced that she was about to close her private school for girls. Once the Rhenish had declined an offer to amalgamate with a new, proposed government institution it was ascertained that there was enough public support and, more important, offers of sponsorship, to ensure the viability of a new government school for girls. Lady teachers were recruited from Mount Holyoke Seminary in America. The first of a number of American ladies to teach at the school included the principal, Miss Juliette Gilson, and her assistant, Miss Carrie Ingraham.

The new school, Bloemhof, occupied the Dorp Street premises lately vacated by the Gymnasium, with Mrs McLachlan's former school building, repaired after a fire, serving as the boarding house. With instruction through the medium of Dutch, the school was soon offering classes from kindergarten to a three-year teacher's course and in time, like the Rhenish, it also accepted 'parlour boarders'. It was Miss Gilson's view that 'in a Colony like this an Education, having reference to the mind alone, seems very deficient'. She therefore introduced a number of practical skills to the curriculum, among them an advanced needlework course which proved the main attraction for the parlour boarders.

In the four years following Miss Gilson's retirement in 1885, there were no fewer than six principals before the arrival of 'Miss Lucy'. Miss Louisa Joubert, born in the district on the farm By-den-Weg, was a niece of the Reverend Johannes Neethling. She arrived during a difficult period of strained relations between Britain and the Boer republics that extended to individuals at local level. With tact and firmness, however, she kept the peace and introduced her own brand of good order and strict discipline. Her girls became their school's finest advertisement, with the result that the enrolment grew rapidly and buildings, including Erfurt House in Ryneveld Street, were acquired to serve as hostels for the boarders. In 1907 the school itself moved to a double-storeyed building in Ryneveld Street that later housed Bloemhof's primary section.

A year later a splendid new building was formally opened in Victoria Street by the governor, Sir Walter Hely-Hutchinson. This was the new home of the Gymnasium which, on the occasion of the move, changed its name to Stellenbosch Boys' High School. As enrolments had advanced, so had academic standards and the range of teaching increased to the stage at which the school and a higher college section were separated. At the time of the move to Victoria Street, the school was under the rectorship of Paul Roos who, in 1906-07, had led the first Springbok rugby team to the British Isles where they had lost only two out of 29 matches. He infused his boys with the same winning spirit, urging them to let their disappointments be stepping stones rather than stumbling blocks. It was Roos who, in 1913, introduced the concept of 'mother-tongue education' at his school, thus making it, perhaps, the first dual-medium school in the country. When, in 1946, it moved across the Eerste River to new premises and the old building became a department of the University, the school was given a new name. Informally but frequently, it had become known as 'Paul Roos's school'; now the name was made official in the title of Paul Roos Gymnasium. In time, both the Rhenish and Bloemhof moved across the river to form a fairly close enclave of education that would both gratify and amaze the succession of men and women who laboured over centuries to achieve it.

THEOLOGICAL SEMINARY AND UNIVERSITY

The creation of the Theological Seminary, which provided the vital impetus to the growth of Stellenbosch as a centre for education, was the ideal of the 1847 Cape Synod of the Dutch Reformed Church. Because of historical trends such as the British occupation of the Cape, the arrival of several thousand British settlers, official prejudice against things and even people un-English, the bias of overseas contact swung away from Holland, the traditional motherland of the Cape. Concerned also for the spiritual welfare of the mostly Dutch-descended Voortrekkers living beyond the church's influence, and desiring to bring Christianity to the indigenous peoples of the interior, the synod determined that 'a theological seminary be established'. Even in 1847 there was still considerable misgiving about a seminary being established at the Cape, and a specially appointed commission failed, in 1855, to attract suitable professors from Holland. Eventually, in 1857 it was announced that the Reverend John Murray of Burgersdorp and the Reverend Nicolaas Hofmeyr of Calvinia had consented to become the first professors of the new institution which had not yet been erected, nor had its site been chosen.

The choice was among Cape Town, Paarl and Stellenbosch. Stellenbosch won because a number of its leading burghers, with the blessing of the entire community, offered to purchase the attractive old drostdy building – and present it free of charge – as a home for the new seminary. Thus, founded in 1858, the Theological Seminary was inaugurated in the former drostdy the following year.

Ten years later, the Theological Seminary was no longer recognizable. Gone was the elegant Cape Dutch façade and in its place stood a dignified building of two storeys containing within it the fabric of the old drostdy. It lasted until 1905 when it was added to without any aesthetic benefit but at least granting much-needed space for the growing number of students. Today the appearance is still basically that of 1905, although much of the cast-iron frill has been removed. The Theological Seminary existed solely for the training of clergy until, with the founding of a Faculty of Theology at the University, the seminary was eventually incorporated with it. The University itself had its origins in the Gymnasium which, like a few other Cape schools, was both school and college.

1874 saw the demise of the Colonial Board of Examiners and the creation of the University of the Cape of Good Hope as the official examining body. At this stage, Dr Langham Dale decided to regard the Gymnasium solely as a school and it was only after a meeting between the Reverend Johannes Neethling and the prime minister, Sir John Molteno, that Dale was persuaded to change his mind. Once officially sanctioned, the college section created an Arts Department under its first full professor, Archibald Macdonald, whose saying it was that instead of reshaping Africa to fit Afrikaners, it was better to shape Afrikaners to fit Africa. What did need reshaping was the building which housed the two sections of the Gymnasium, so an extra wing was added to the old slave school cum smallpox hospital. Despite a measure of physical 'togetherness' for a while, school and college formally acquired separate identities in 1881 as the Stellenbosch College and the Stellenbosch Gymnasium. By then, a magnificent new building was arising to the design of Carl Otto Hager who produced for the occasion an impressive classical façade. Or did he? According to at least one reputable authority the design is not Hager's but that of R M Robertson who was responsible for rebuilding the Theological Seminary in 1905. But whoever designed it, the Ou Hoofgebou, now a National Monument, is still a credit to the town and University. It was when this new building was about to be inaugurated in 1887, the year of Queen Victoria's Golden Jubilee, that Dr Dale suggested it might be appropriate to change the name of Stellenbosch College to Queen's College. This was amended to Victoria College and the royal assent was duly obtained.

Senior school pupils continued to attend Victoria College until 1899 when it became a 'proper' university, still carrying its old title. The change from Victoria College to University of Stellenbosch was brought about by an Act of Parliament that took effect on 2 April 1918, creating also the University of Cape Town and the University of South Africa. As the University has grown so it has spread, with the main campus concentrated between the Banhoek Road and Victoria Street, and between Andringa Street and Cluver Road.

All painted up and apparently going nowhere, this old car
was a hostel's contribution to brightening up the town.

*'What would Mevrouw Schreuder have heard,
for instance, as she stood at her open hearth…'*

THE PAST PRESERVED

IT MAY OCCUR TO ANYONE who knows far-away Pilgrim's Rest, that Stellenbosch, like the little eastern Transvaal mining town of yesteryear, is its own museum. There are immense differences of course, in architecture, period and ambience, but each wears its past proudly and unselfconsciously, even endearingly. But apart from the magic of its streets with their fascination of façades, Stellenbosch has a special collection of buildings that together form a designated repository of the past – the Village Museum. This is a place that allows you to make the journey from the Stellenbosch that was actually little more than a rough clearing with only a sprinkle of humble buildings, through eras of increasing prosperity and sophistication, to relatively recent times.

The start is Schreuderhuis which was on its present site and in its present form – so far as can be determined – in February of the year 1710. This makes it certainly the oldest domestic structure in Stellenbosch and, probably, the oldest in the European tradition in the entire country. It was built by a German immigrant named Sebastian Schröder, whose name was habitually written by the scribes of the Dutch East India Company as Sebastiaan Schreuder, which is its Dutch form. It was probably to this little house, on 9 March 1710, that Schreuder brought his new bride, Sara Wijnsandt of Amsterdam, whom he had just married in the little church of which the foundations may still be seen beneath D'Ouwe Werf, round the corner in Church Street. It is a simple home with simple implements and utensils that date from the years 1690 to 1720. Floorboards, like window glass, came later, especially in the case of the humbler citizen. Glass travelled badly in the holds of the Company's ships so, when it was sent at all, it was in the form of small squares or diamonds. Creating a window of these fragments meant the use of lead which, even then, was an expensive metal. So the Schreuders, like so many others, made do with oiled cloth in the window spaces. Especially on bright days, when the outside glare is harsh, it gives a wonderfully gentle light to the interior.

There is just one thing missing from this house and, inevitably, from any home that is a period museum – the sounds of the times. What would Mevrouw Schreuder have heard, for instance, as she stood at her open hearth or carefully swept the floor with the

Left *Part of the fascination of old things is working out their purpose.*

Above *This early fire-engine is little more than a hand-operated pump.*

sunlight slanting in at her door? Perhaps the creak of slow wagon wheels, the sound of the rims on the ground muffled by the soft earth and the snorting of oxen. Perhaps she would have heard wind rippling the leaves of young oak trees, the familiar cackle and fidget of her hens in the kitchen garden and the distant calling of voices. And certainly in winter there would have been the loud rush of the waters of the Eerste River – there were two channels then – as they tumbled the rounded stones along their course to the sea. This was a pioneer's home and it stood as the furthest bastion of European culture in this remote corner of Africa. Think about Schreuderhuis when it was new, or almost new, and of the life then within it and around it, and hear the sounds.

Now we move through the garden – and time – towards Bletterman House. It faces on to Plein Street and we enter by the back door, but even that is grander than the entrance to most houses. This is a classic of the H-shaped house, with a total of six gables – front and rear, and a gable at each end of both arms of the H. It was built in about 1789 for Hendrik Bletterman who, as the landdrost, was a man of some means. He was also a man of some versatility because, when his services as landdrost were no longer required, he turned his talents or, at any rate, his attention, to running a tailoring business. Whether he wielded needle and scissors himself, or used slaves or paid workers, we do not know, but it is entertaining to picture his clients calling to be fitted. Since most

Left *Preoccupied with their bicycles, these schoolboys are probably unaware that Sir Herbert Baker designed the cottages behind them in the style known as Cape Dutch Revival. They serve now as the Oude Meester Brandy Museum.*

Right *This immense and ancient grape-press draws attention to the Stellenryck Wine Museum. Once it housed the cellar of Libertas Parva, home of the Krige family.*

Above *Like a shimmering little palace of crystal, a display of glass at the Stellenryck Wine Museum both scatters and concentrates the light of a chandelier.*

Right *Was life itself three centuries ago any less complicated for the simplicity of everyday artefacts like those seen here in the kitchen of Schreuderhuis? It's tempting to think that it was, but the same range and play of emotions have been a part of us since Creation.*

of the clothing he is on record as having made was fairly rough stuff – uniforms for the mounted police, for example – one imagines that they, like us, would have come to the back door for the fitting-room would surely have been closest to it. By 1858 Bletterman House had become the magistrate's court, and so it would remain for a century or more. When Bletterman House was being restored as part of the Village Museum, a parcel of dynamite was found beneath the floors of the former police station next door. In the belief that old dynamite was harmless, it was robustly handled and slapped about until someone knowledgeable pointed out that it is, in fact, extremely unstable and still highly explosive. Where it came from is unknown, and where it might have blown the new Village Museum is also unknown, the fates having decided to be kind.

They have been kind, too, to Grosvenor House, with its elegant double-storeyed façade. Look above the door for the little palm tree, in relief, which has become the emblem of the Village Museum. It goes back a long way and in Psalm 92: 12 we read that 'the righteous shall flourish like a palm tree'. Grosvenor House was built, probably in conventional Cape Dutch style, in about 1782, by a German named Nöthing, a surname that, in time, became Neethling. Later owners, of whom two others were German, altered the house until, by 1803, it had achieved its present appearance. There is a lovely garden at the back – lovely in its formal simplicity of old-fashioned herbs, roses and viburnum, camellias and clivias, and a rustic seat almost buried beneath a tangle of trailing honeysuckle. Turkeys, ducks and fowls co-exist here peacefully if sometimes fairly vocally, and just over the hedge is the serene bulk of the Moederkerk. This is probably the most tranquil garden in Stellenbosch.

The long building at right-angles to Grosvenor House and fronting on Van Riebeeck Street (a continuation of Plein Street) houses a collection of antique toys, some unrelentingly patriotic or stolidly educational, others frivolous. Grosvenor House itself is a stately place, furnished in the style of around 1830 with a solemnity that dissipates entirely in the garden.

We cross the road, and the gurgling water in the furrow, to reach what was once the home of Oloff Bergh, whose name it still bears although it was also the home of, among others, Professor John Murray of the nearby Theological Seminary. Oloff Bergh House was once a typical H-shaped, single-storeyed dwelling in the Cape Dutch tradition, although this may be hard to discern today. For one thing, although the entrance is now in Drostdy Street, it used to be around the corner in Church Street. The present front door leads into a passage that once was the space between the arms of the H where, when these were external walls, there were built-in nesting-boxes for the poultry, a feature now seen only in some Boland farmyards.

Another feature, one that you may notice as you study the present front facade before entering, is the drip-moulds above the windows. In the days of dusty, untarred streets the external walls of houses often became covered with a layer of dust stirred by wind or the passage of animals and vehicles. It was washed off by rain, and the drip-moulds – the horizontal projections above the windows and door – prevented the dust-laden water from flowing over and streaking the glass. At any rate, that was the theory and, even if it did not work, drip-moulds make an attractive feature. The furnishing of Oloff Bergh House is in the style of the mid-19th century, when Victorian clutter was becoming fashionable but had not yet reached the scrambled interior hysteria that was so much in evidence later.

Across town on the edge of the Braak – the first National Monument to be proclaimed in Stellenbosch – is the old arsenal or kruithuis, itself proclaimed a few years later, in 1940. With the 'eye' of its bell tower seemingly turned to the side, its shape is slightly reminiscent of the old-fashioned laundry iron known as 'omkykertjie', which means 'little one looking back'. Look for one of these devices in the Village Museum. It is a cast-iron affair with a hinged top that was raised to insert the hot coals. Once the lid is closed and secured, the chimney of the iron rises a short distance and then turns to the side so that hot air from the inside will not burn the operator's hand. To return to the kruithuis, which flies the flag of the Dutch East India Company… Here are cannons, cannon barrels, uniforms, swords and, most impressive of all, the old muzzle-loading muskets. You needed to be fairly robust merely to hold one and keep it pointed in the right direction.

Look at one of the flintlocks: on the side is the cock holding the piece of flint in its jaws. When the trigger is pulled, it strikes against the steel frizzen, the curved piece of metal hinged at the front of the lock-plate. This contact sends a shower of sparks into the little pan below and some of the sparks find their way through a tiny hole drilled in the barrel, there to ignite the main charge of gunpowder and send the bullet – a ball of lead – on its wobbly and inaccurate path. Hitting even the side of a barn beyond a range of about 100 m was merely coincidental. All the same, the modern rifle consists of exactly the same basic components – lock, stock and barrel. Having studied the simple construction and intricate operation of a smoothbore flintlock musket, it is easy to appreciate the skill required to hit the parrot at the annual *kermis* or festival. This event gave its name to Papegaaiberg, the high hill overlooking the town from the west, although, naturally, the parrot was not a live bird. Some accounts say it was made of wood, others of metal, but all agree it was mounted on a pole on top of Papegaaiberg. The first parrot-shoot was held in 1686 and the marksmen, having paid an entry fee, took up position at a range of 19 m from the parrot and fired in turn. Prizes were awarded according to the particular part of the parrot that was shot off, with the main prize of 25 rix dollars going to the shottist who, by hitting an area of the tail, destroyed the target completely. If the parrot survived, the prize money was doubled and held over until the following year when, presumably, a fresh parrot was brought out. Why a parrot? There's much to muse on in museums...

There are other museums, too. Also on the edge of the Braak is Burgherhuis, headquarters of Historical Homes of South Africa Limited where several rooms open to the public have on display treasures of furniture, glass and porcelain. Carl Otto Hager's little Lutheran church in Dorp Street is home of the art collection of the University of Stellenbosch. Down at the other end of Dorp Street is the old Krige homestead, Klein Libertas or Libertas Parva, which, restored to its simple splendour, has now become the Rembrandt van Rijn Art Gallery. The outbuild-

ing, probably once the wine cellar, contains fascinating exhibits of the Stellenryck Wine Museum while much in evidence outside is an immense wooden wine-press, reminiscent in its bulk and outline of some ancient Roman machine of war. Old Strand Road runs its short course at the side of Klein Libertas, coming to an end outside elegant cottages built, it is said, to a design by the eminent architect Herbert Baker. Today they house the Oude Meester Brandy Museum.

Slightly further afield, at Vlottenburg, is the Van Ryn Brandy Cellar and Cooperage where even those who do not like brandy will be fascinated by its story on a tour of the distillery and maturation cellars. Here too, you may see a cooper at work practising techniques that are more ancient than we know. Certainly they are more ancient than those required to make the items that have replaced the old casks and barrels and, in so doing, have killed or cramped the skills acquired only by long and patient practice and masterly co-ordination of hand and eye. Once, there were coopers in almost every town of the western Cape Province; there were wheelwrights and farriers, blacksmiths and carpenters, men who earned their living by the sweat of their brow and the skilled strength of their hands. They attained a quality, if not a precision, beyond any that can be achieved by machine. And, in the hastening way of the world, they are gone.

But still there is Stellenbosch.

These antelope, poised in bronze amid their garden setting,
are to be seen at the Stellenryck Wine Museum.

*'...roads, like cords casually dropped
on a green, crumpled quilt...'*

AMONG THE VINES

THE STORY OF WINE runs close to the story of the Cape itself for it started when Jan van Riebeeck, commander of the little settlement, first planted vines in 1655. Although he dutifully praised the Lord when wine was made four years later, it was not, according to the Company officials who tasted it, of a very good quality. It took an influx of French refugees, a few of whom knew something of the vine and of winemaking, and an enthusiast like Simon van der Stel, to make solid the shaky foundations laid by Van Riebeeck. It took, too, development of the fertile valleys and slopes of the winelands, each with its own particular micro-climate, accompanied by a remarkable advance in technology, to establish the Cape – and Stellenbosch in particular – unquestionably as a home of fine wines.

No matter how you approach the town – and there are several roads, like cords casually dropped on a green, crumpled quilt – you will pass, first of all, through its vineyards. An enlightening way to see them is to take the Wine Route, the creation, in 1971, of three local farmers. In its office in Strand Road, just about 600 m from the Dorp Street intersection, there are maps and other brochures that will ensure that you are well equipped to savour the outing to the full. In fact, if you are to do justice to either the route or its wines, or to both, you will want to take the Stellenbosch Wine Route more than once.

Let's start out west for the Polkadraai Road, with its sweeping bend named after the vigorous 19th-century dance so beloved of the old-time country folk, which leads us soon to the entrance to Neethlingshof. Now, pines, unlike the spreading, deciduous oak, are rarely impressive at the Cape. This is an opinion instantly revised as one approaches the long pine avenue that takes us, like the aisle of some outdoor cathedral, to Neethlingshof. In fact, so spectacular is it that its depiction has been used on the estate's label. Neethlingshof dates from 1699, and the lovely Cape Dutch gabled homestead from about 1819. New additions, including a cellar, are designed to blend with the old but are uncompromisingly modern in function. The Lord Neethling Restaurant, named after a former owner said to have had pretensions to grandeur (and who can blame him, in this setting?), specializes in Chinese cuisine but also offers Continental and traditional Cape dishes – indoors or, in the summer months,

Left *Morgenhof estate – oaks and furrows,
vines and, always, the mountains.*

Above *A carriage ride on Blaauwklippen is one
of the treats of the Stellenbosch Wine Route.*

on the Palm Terrace. Both premium cultivars (from 'cultivated variety') and blended wines are produced, the estate's 1990 Rhine Riesling Noble Late Harvest having received the award for South African Champion Wine for that year.

Leading westwards from the Polkadraai Road, just beyond Neethlingshof, is the road to Stellenbosch Kloof which passes the farm Overgaauw. It is worth noting that in 1883 an Abraham van Velden of Overgaauw was one of the earliest graduates of the Stellenbosch School of Agriculture, later Elsenburg Agricultural College. A later namesake maintains the tradition as owner and winemaker today, both white and red wines of Overgaauw having been sold at the renowned annual Nederburg auctions of rare Cape wines.

Further into the Kloof is a very old estate indeed, one that was once the outermost ward of Stellenbosch and so came to be named Uiterwyk. The homestead which dates from 1791 (although the farm was granted more than a century before that) is one of the classics of Cape Dutch architecture, the complex curves of its gable peeping through the summer green of sheltering oaks. The De Waal family has been farming here since 1912 but is reputed to have started agricultural operations 300 years ago in the vicinity of Cape Town's Wale or Waal Street. There is an old cellar where red wines mature in oak vats and a new cellar where the tasting-room offers, among other cultivars, the unique Müller-Thurgau.

Saxenburg lies close to the bend that gave its name to Polkadraai Road, its vineyards spread high on the hills above the Kuils River. The grant of land here was made in 1693 and old buildings – although not as old as the grant – were being restored in 1992 to serve as a restaurant. Formerly specializing

in whites, the estate has recently started producing an impressive range of red wines as well.

Swinging south-west from the Polkadraai Road just a few kilometres out of Stellenbosch, and just before the entrance to Neethlingshof, the modern road R310 closely follows the old track along the valley of the Eerste River through some of the earliest farmlands of the district. Vredenheim wine estate is on Vredenburg farm which was granted in 1692 and boasts a grand Cape Dutch homestead built in 1789. It boasts, too, one of the few lady winemakers in the country and, in 1992, the only one on the Wine Route. A short distance from Vredenheim is Vlottenburg Co-operative Winery where, annually, some 12 000 tonnes of grapes are pressed to yield 10 million litres of wine. The extensive range includes two rare wines – Gamay Noir, a light red, and Muscat de Hambourg, a sweet red dessert wine. Eersterivier-valleise Ko-op, whose cellar-master received the Diner's Club Wine Maker of the Year Award in 1984 for his Sauvignon Blanc, is almost next door. Grapes are received from Devon Valley, Vlottenburg, Lynedoch, Vlaeberg and Helderberg, and a large range of wines is produced.

At Spier, you can sample not only the excellence of wines, but the glories of Cape Dutch architecture at various stages of its flowering. Such a variety of magnificent gables will not be seen on any other single farm, so take your time to enjoy them before going into a restaurant (there are two) or tasting-room. A very full range includes several sparkling wines as well as dessert wines. Close neighbour to Spier is Welmoed Co-operative Wine Cellars. They take their name from the farm Welmoed, granted by Simon van der Stel in 1690 to Henning Hüsing, later a stern opponent of the younger Van der Stel. The

Right *Pines and gum trees form windbreaks for manicured fields and vineyards that extend to the gentle, lower mountain slopes.*

Far left *A plaque at gracious old Muratie tells part of the story of the farm's ownership from the time it was granted in 1685.*

Left *The cellar of the Franschhoek Vineyards Co-operative has a classical facade, quite unlike the Cape Dutch styles that surround it.*

co-op is much more recent and in the 50 years of its existence has gained an enviable number of awards for its many wines. A restaurant is open all year round.

From Stellenbosch, Strand Road runs south to the sea, passing a number of Wine Route farms on its way. The first of these is Blaauwklippen on the Dwarsrivier or Blaauwklip stream. This is another very early grant; it goes back to 1690 although the oldest building, the *jonkershuis* or home traditionally occupied by the eldest son, dates from 1780. It was built by Dirk Hoffman, son of a former landdrost and, needing space to accommodate his grand total of 22 children, he is thought also to have erected the main homestead. An 'old Cape' museum and coach rides through the vineyards are attractions additional to tasting the excellent wines.

Rust en Vrede is a marvellous name that does indeed conjure up a vision of rest and content, but the wonderful vistas of the Helderberg Mountains come as a bonus. Three Cape Dutch buildings date back to 1780, although the original homestead has become the *jonkershuis*, and the present homestead was once the wagon-house. The original cellar, however, remained the cellar although a new one has been built for the production of the farm's red wines, of which only four are produced from the 30 or so hectares of vines.

A change from the style of Cape Dutch greets one at Eikendal where the winery in the modern Californian idiom does not seem at all out of place on the slopes of the Helderberg. Reds and whites are made here from slow-ripening grapes cooled by breezes from nearby False Bay. Avontuur or 'adventure' is

an exciting name for a new winery located almost opposite the turn into Winery Road that leads to Firgrove. Several places called Avontuur in the Cape were really originally named 'avond uur' or 'evening hour', but this estate, where thoroughbred horses are also bred, is too recent for there to have been any such confusion. The winner of the 1989 'Durban July' came from Avontuur! Along Winery Road is De Helderberg Co-operative, founded in 1905 and so one of the oldest co-operative wine cellars in the country. All grapes processed here are grown close by, and red and white wines, sparkling wine, fortified wines and grape juice are produced.

Red wines alone are the speciality of the wine estate reputed to be the smallest in Stellenbosch, with just six hectares under vines. This is Clos Malverne which is reached by turning back towards Stellenbosch and taking the Devon Valley Road, a pretty drive through gentle hills below Papegaaiberg. Another drive with fine views over lower-lying countryside is the Helshoogte Road on the far side of Stellenbosch from Devon Valley. Despite its ominous-sounding name, the route is a perfectly easy one all on excellent tar. Here, near the summit of the pass, is the estate of Delaire which refers to itself, with some justification, as the 'vineyards in the sky'. Views of the surrounding mountain ranges are quite superb and can be enjoyed from the estate's tasting-room where wines, principally whites, are offered.

Oude Nektar lies on the road to Jonkershoek, albeit before it has gained the summit on its winding way through shady trees. The massive but finely proportioned gable of the house known as Old Nectar rises above the greenery to announce the presence of a farm that was originally granted – to two freed slaves – in 1692. A vast dam reflects sky and mountains, and is an attraction for many species of waterbirds and those who watch them. Oude Nektar wine estate, as distinct from the homestead from which it is now separated, has undergone many changes since a change of ownership in 1989, but a range of excellent wines is available.

For another voyage of discovery and wine appreciation, you can leave Stellenbosch on the north-bound Klapmuts Road (R44). Historic buildings have been restored and vineyards replanted with noble cultivars at Morgenhof, just a few kilometres from town on the foothills of the Simonsberg. There is a well-established herb garden (and another at the Village Museum) and you can also enjoy the estate's 'boutique style' wines. A little road leads up the slopes of the Simonsberg to an estate that has an aura of almost fairytale loveliness and a name to ponder over – Muratie. (In this, as in many Dutch

Left *Schoongezicht is the home not only of very fine wine, but also of this champion Jersey herd, one of the first of the breed to be established in the country. The farm, with a history going back almost 300 years, was once owned by John X Merriman, the last Prime Minister of the old Cape Colony.*

Right *Avontuur winery, which combines the latest technology with the best of traditions, is overlooked by the Helderberg range. Apart from winemaking, the rearing of thoroughbred horses is one of the estate's activities.*

words, the 't' in this position is pronounced as an 's'.) Muratie means 'ruin' and may refer to the long-vanished remains of an earlier structure on what is claimed as the oldest private wine estate in the country, dating back to 1685. This was the first estate to cultivate Pinot Noir, some vintages of which have appeared on offer at the Nederburg auction. Muratie's 1990 Port won a gold medal at the SA Young Wine Show two years after extensive replanting began on the estate.

On up the road beyond Muratie lies an estate that offers some of the finest views in the winelands – Delheim. This was once the old farm De Driesprongh, home of the gunner – the ruins of whose house may still be seen – responsible for firing the signal cannon on the nearby Kanonkop. The wines of Delheim – and there is an impressively large selection – have garnered many awards. A light lunch is available throughout the year – a vintner's platter in summer and country soup in

the winter months. Lower on the slopes of Simonsberg is Lievland where the building that has now become the tasting centre has an unusual winged and pedimented gable dated 1823 when the farm is believed to have been called Beyerskloof. An indomitable little European baroness, whose husband bought the estate in the 1930s and then died soon after, was for many years the moving force behind the running of the farm, making the wines herself. Since then the vineyards have been replanted and it is worth noting that a later winemaker on Lievland was also a lady who subsequently moved to her own estate at Tulbagh.

Turning back towards Stellenbosch and then into the Kromme Rhee Road, we reach Simonsig, one of the largest of the private estates. Here, the first sparkling wine in South Africa to be made by the original *méthode Champenoise* – that is, by bottle fermentation – was produced on a commercial scale.

Above *Gaunt in their beauty, a row of pines separates a production vineyard from one where groundcover grows between the vines on Delheim estate.*

Right *It's harvest time. Strong hands and shoulders carry baskets of luscious grapes to a trailer that, when filled with a mountain of goodness, will be towed away to the winery.*

Note that South African sparkling wine is never referred to as 'Champagne', nor do South African wines ever assume French place-names such as Bordeaux or Burgundy. This is by a special agreement with the French Government made in the 1930s. The Simonsig range extends far beyond sparkling wines, though, and many of its products have won wide acclaim.

Beyond the intersection with the Koelenhof Road lies Hartenberg estate granted in 1704 to Christoffel Extreux (whose surname later became Esterhuizen) though the homestead with its somewhat severe 'square' gable dates from 1849. In addition to a range of cultivar and blended wines, there are also three house wines that are available only at the estate. Lunch is offered throughout the year – in winter in the tasting-room, and in summer in the green peace of the garden. Hartenberg is in the area known as Bottelary which takes its name from that of the provisions store aboard ships of the Dutch East India Company. Why the name was given to this area is not clear but it accounts for the naming of the Bottelary Co-operative Winery and the labels on its very full range of wines depict the bottelary aboard an old-time sailing ship.

THE RURAL FOUNDATION

A happy innovation in this area is harvest day, the last Saturday of February, when visitors may join in the picking and pressing of the grapes. This is the most memorable time of the year when the air is rich with the robust fragrance of early fermentation and the vineyards are not simply fields planted with vines but workplaces where men and women labour long, hard hours under the sun. What is the lot of the farm labourer in today's winelands? The answer must be that it varies according to the degree of caring or compassionate understanding shown by the employer and one of the ways in which he can show his concern is by becoming affiliated with the Rural Foundation which has its headquarters in Stellenbosch. This is an organization founded in the late 1980s to provide guidance and leadership in the development of rural communities – and each farm is its own micro-community – 'to create a better future for all people in rural areas in southern Africa'. It aims at promoting a community life that is healthy, both physically and spiritually, through involvement in self-care and the attainment of peace and justice for all rural people. In practical terms it includes the arrangement of pre-school care for the children of farm workers, primary health care, the improvement of living conditions through, for instance, the electrification of cottages. Sport and recreation and the improvement of adult literacy are among other concerns.

Left *Middelvlei estate has wonderful views of the mighty Stellenbosch mountains.*

Right *Labels are affixed by hand on Muratie's wine bottles.*

Above *A traditional delicacy, waterblommetjies are enjoying a revival of popularity, although harvesting them looks a chilly undertaking.*

Right *This harvest of rich red strawberries has been gathered on Polkadraai Farm.*

By far the greatest number of the Rural Foundation's affiliates come from the western Cape. They represent only some 300 000 of South Africa's farm workers, computed at around 1,32 million people in all. However, numbers are growing, and the Rural Foundation has been described as 'a story of hope for the future'.

THE WINE BOFFINS

Most wine farmers themselves have undergone rigorous training in classroom, vineyard and cellar. To provide a firm academic grounding for them, the Department of Oenology and Viticulture was established at the University of Stellenbosch in 1917 and, since then, has played an important part in the successful development of the industry. Co-operation and the interchange of ideas and results is international, and particularly strong relationships have been formed with such institutions as the Davis Campus of the University of California and the Long Ashton Research Centre in Avon, England.

Of immeasurable help to the wine industry is the Oenological and Viticultural Research Institute (OVRI) at Nietvoorbij, situated just north of Stellenbosch and an offshoot of the Department of Agriculture. Research into all aspects of the vine and wine production is undertaken, with satellite stations in other wine-growing regions, such as Orange River and Klein Karoo. Imported stocks are quarantined and evaluated at Nietvoorbij where wine-cellar technology, in all its aspects, is also studied.

Legislation in 1972 brought about a new concept of the term 'estate'. Until then it had been loosely used to refer to any wine farm that was spacious in extent and gracious in its lifestyle – no matter whether it made wine from its own grapes or bought them in from elsewhere. Now, in order to claim the title 'estate', a wine farm had to produce its wine solely from grapes grown within its own boundaries.

THE BIG THREE

Farmers who do not make their own wine in their own cellars have a choice of various co-operatives and wine companies to which they can send their grapes. In Stellenbosch the 'big three' in the wine industry are Stellenbosch Farmers' Winery, the Oude Meester Group and Gilbey Distillers and Vintners.

Reputed to produce more than half the volume of wine consumed in South Africa, Stellenbosch Farmers' Winery has its headquarters at Oude Libertas, on the Eerste River. Once it was part of the farm owned by Adam Tas, sharp-tongued commentator on affairs of his day, who acquired it, name and all, in 1703 by marrying a well-to-do widow. In time, Oude

Left *It is first light, and already a tractor, tiny in the distance, growls as it works on the fields of Alto estate. Later the fields, cool and shady now with their protective borders of robust trees, will shimmer in the noonday heat.*

Above *A long road, and a dusty one, winds through the autumn vineyards on Kanonkop.*

Libertas came into the possession of the Krige family who established a winery and distillery and, as a form of insurance against ill fortune, also farmed ostriches, mushrooms and whatever else might flourish. In the event, the Kriges had little success and by 1924 matters looked grim.

In that year, an American settler at the Cape, having previously been declared insolvent, was formally rehabilitated. He was William Charles Winshaw, who appears to have had a remarkable career. Born in Kentucky in 1872, he ran away from home before reaching his teens and led a Huckleberry Finn sort of existence before becoming a gold prospector, law man, gambler and, surprisingly, a medical doctor. But quiet country practice was not for him, and he arrived in Table Bay at the start of the South African War in charge of a large consignment of mules for the British army. His first glimpse of Stellenbosch came when he handed over his charges at the remount depot there, returning a few years later to live as a tenant on the farm Patrys Vlei. After early experiments that involved his wife's kitchen stove, in 1909 Winshaw started the Stellenbosch Grape Juice Works where he produced both wine and unfermented juice, his ideal being to make a good, natural wine 'for the working man'. After becoming part-owner of the Stellenbosch Distillery, Winshaw went on to many other related ventures – too many of them – and in 1921 he was declared insolvent. He returned to the United States for a few years but, early in 1924 and now aged 52, he was back in Stellenbosch, entering into partnership with Gideon Krige of Oude Libertas and buying him out a few years later.

Although times were hard, Winshaw was not merely an optimist, but an energetic one. In 1930 there appeared Grand

Left *Something has attracted these egrets to share the company of some fine-looking pigs on a farm near Franschhoek.*

Right *There is mist in the valleys and sunlight on the peaks of the Franschhoek mountains as a new day dawns over Delheim, an estate lying high on the slopes of the Simonsberg.*

Mousseux, still one of the leading sparkling wines. Later followed La Gratitude, a dry white wine named after the house Winshaw had bought in Dorp Street, and a dry red wine called Chateau Libertas which perpetuated the name of the old estate. Other wines which recalled old Adam Tas, once a wine farmer himself, included Tasheimer, Oom Tas and, perhaps most famous of all, Tassenberg. Winshaw's enterprise grew and in 1935 became a public company, laying the basis for the formation of Stellenbosch Farmers' Winery. Mergers saw it become the owner of Monis of Paarl, which brought the renowned Nederburg winery into the corporate fold. In 1970 came the takeover of the long-established firm of Sedgwick-Taylor, thus increasing the company's share in the market for spirits and fortified wines.

One of the most remarkable success stories, and a tribute to those who developed it at the right time, was a semi-sweet white wine made largely from Chenin Blanc. Called Lieberstein, it was launched in 1959 and 30 000 litres were sold. Five years later more than 30 *million* litres of Lieberstein were sold, not in total, but in the single year of 1964. It was only in 1962 – at the age of 92 – that William Winshaw retired from active business, leaving the running of the company to his son Bill.

A tour of the vast premises at Oude Libertas is one of the highlights of a visit to the winelands. Just across the road from

Left *Here, being harvested by brightly dressed Xhosa women, is yet another Stellenbosch crop – broccoli.*

Above *Scarecrows guard the strawberries on a farm near Stellenbosch where a vivid and creative imagination has been given free rein.*

Right *Women at work in the vegetable fields along the Vlaeberg Road. Although renowned for its wines, the good earth of Stellenbosch yields an impressive range of produce.*

Left *Before the sun has quite gone, an early rising moon peeps through a cleft in the Simonsberg.*

Below *Late autumn vines add muted colour as grey clouds drift about the peaks of the Helderberg.*

the winery is the Oude Libertas Complex, set in a sea of vines. Standard roses planted at the end of each row of vines can be seen from the road and continue a tradition that began in the days of the horse-drawn plough. It is said that particularly thorny roses were chosen so that, in rounding the end of each row, the horse would avoid taking too close a turn and in this way ensure that the implement it drew would not damage the vines. Another reason given for planting roses in vineyards in bygone times was that if fungus or rot were to strike the vines, it might well affect the roses first and so give the farmer some advance warning and, perhaps, time to ward off disaster. Whether these theories are true or not does not really matter but the roses make for a pretty display of colour against the green of the vines. The Oude Libertas Complex in their midst includes a cellar and restaurant, and an open-air amphitheatre where a variety of international and local performers find an appreciative audience under the oaks and the stars.

One of the best-known names in South African industry is that of Dr Anton Rupert and it was he who, at the height of the chaos and uncertainty of the Second World War, founded a company which was to become another of the giants of the wine industry. A young university lecturer at the time, he had faith enough in the future to form a very small investment company with a partner. Over the following years it continued to develop until in 1945 Distillers Corporation (SA) Limited was registered. The first of its pot-stills and a modern wine analytical laboratory, the only one of its kind in South Africa at the time, were ready for use the following year. Soon a full range of grape products was being marketed, the best known of them being Oude Meester and Richelieu brandy.

Above *Boschendal is dwarfed by the Drakenstein Mountains that provide the incomparably lovely homestead with a dramatic setting. Described as being in the Cape Flemish style, the house was completed in 1812, when wine had been made here for almost a century.*

Right *Seemingly about to be engulfed by surrounding vineyards, a simple cottage near Franschhoek is snug beneath its trees.*

Marketing agreements were entered into with private estates, Alto and Theuniskraal being the first in 1947. During the 1960s the Drostdy Co-operative Cellars of Tulbagh, the largest private sherry maturation cellars in the country, were taken over and soon afterwards Distillers en Brouerskorporasie, parent company of Oude Meester Kelders was founded. In 1968 work started on implementing one of Dr Rupert's most inspired ideas: the building of The Bergkelder, which involved tunnelling deep into the southern face of Papegaaiberg to create a vast cellar. Magnificently carved oak vats are a feature of the Bergkelder where, in addition to maturing its own products under optimal conditions, space is also reserved for clients to store their special wines. Bergkelder's own wines include the Fleur du Cap, Stellenryck and Grünberger ranges.

In 1970 came the merger with South African Distilleries and Wines Limited, a group composed of some 40 wine merchants, some of whom, such as E K Green and Collison's, had taken root as long ago as the 19th century. Four years later followed the announcement that several leading private wine estates had entered into marketing agreements with the Bergkelder on the basis of those already existing with Alto and Theuniskraal. These estate owners would continue to make their own wines but they would now be bottled and distributed by the Bergkelder, at the same time benefiting from its advanced technology. By 1989 the group included some 19 farmers from wine estates in the regions of Stellenbosch, Durbanville, Tulbagh, Robertson and Swartland.

The third of the three giant wine companies based in Stellenbosch is Gilbey Distillers and Vintners. It had its origins

Far left *The Huguenot Monument and adjacent museum at Franschhoek commemorate the contribution to their new land by these hardy French pioneers.*

Left *Paarl and the valley of the Berg River form an enchanting panorama from the Wiesenhof lookout point.*

Above *Above Paarl, a town that has claims to having been the nurturing place of Afrikaans, the Taalmonument soars skywards.*

as long ago as 1857 when two London wine importers, Walter and Alfred Gilbey, added Cape wines and brandy to their stock in trade, advertising the wine at £1 and the brandy at £1 10s a dozen. Even for that distant time the prices were low and made possible in part by the fact that no excise was levied on colonial produce. This happy state of affairs came to an end soon afterwards when the British Government withdrew the preferential tariff. Many Cape farmers were obliged to sell up and leave but Gilbeys survived.

Trade soon became a two-way enterprise, with Continental spirits, especially gin, being exported to South Africa until, in 1950, after almost a century of association, W & A Gilbey established a distillery at Pietermaritzburg, initially to produce the first of the locally made London gins. Further expansion followed in 1962 with the acquisition of R Santhagens, brandy producer and wine merchant of Stellenbosch. René Santhagen, a civil engineer and scientist, had come to South Africa in the 1890s to run Sammy Marks's famous Hatherley Distillery at Eerste Fabrieken in the Transvaal. During the South African War Santhagen returned to Europe where he improved his knowledge of distilling but on his return to Pretoria after hostilities had ended he discovered that his former employment no longer existed. Santhagen then accepted an offer from Stellenbosch wine farmer and businessman, W A Krige, to join him. A few years later, with the brothers J and C Marais, he started importing the most modern equipment available and established the Golden Lion Distillery at Vlottenburg. Meanwhile gold magnate Sir Lionel Phillips was so impressed with a very fine brandy that Santhagen had made that he financed him in buying the historic Oude Molen in Stellenbosch and so enabled him to go into business entirely on his own account. An Irish surveyor named Dwyer undertook the marketing of the product, known as Santy's Brandy, and soon it was well known throughout the country. Dwyer set up his own company which, after the Second World War, amalgamated with Santhagen's to become Dwyer Santhagens Distilleries.

In 1962 Gilbeys acquired this company, making their headquarters at De Oude Molen, which had in the past not only been the offices of René Santhagen but the very gracious home that he shared with his wife, Emilie. The company existed as Gilbey-Santhagens until 1970 when the name was changed to Gilbey Distillers and Vintners. It was at this time that the wine farm, De Kleine Zalze on the Strand Road, was purchased, and it is here that many of the wines are made.

Another major acquisition was that of Bertram's Wines Limited, in 1972. This company had been founded in the late 19th century, after R F Bertram had bought the estate High Constantia – now named Schoenstatt and the home of a religious order. In time, a full range of wines was marketed under the name of Bertram's of Constantia, but the pressures of urban expansion seriously disrupted farming in the valley, particularly after the Second World War. When Bertram's was bought by Simeon Blumberg in 1959 he moved the centre of operations to the large farm he already owned at Devon Valley, near Stellenbosch and, after a further change of ownership, the merger with Gilbey Distillers and Vintners followed. The Devon Valley centre today includes a distillery and winery where an immense range of grape products originates.

The granite domes of Paarl – known as Britannia,
Gordon and Paarl rocks – form a prominent landmark.